Our story of the Sensational Nightingales (Gales) revolves around three principal protagonists – Jo Jo (Joseph) Wallace who joined the second line-up in 1952 and remains in the group to this day; Rev. Julius (June) Cheeks who joined the first group in 1951 and quit for the Gospel Knights in 1959; and Charles Johnson who permanently replaced Cheeks in 1962 and left to form the Revivers twenty years later.

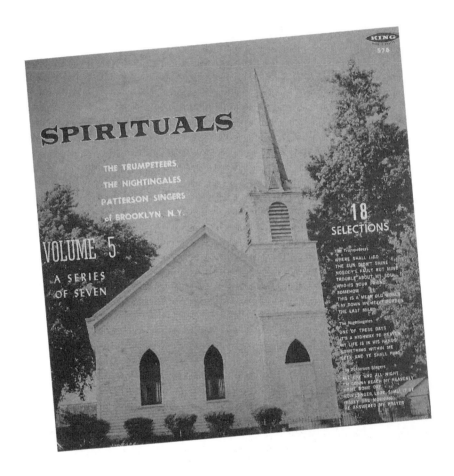

"Spirituals" – King LP 576

Sensational Nightingales

The Story of Joseph "Jo Jo" Wallace
and the Early Days of the
Sensational Nightingales

Opal Louis Nations

Black Scat Books

2014

Sensational Nightingales:
The Story of Joseph "Jo Jo" Wallace &
the Early Days of the Sensational Nightingales

by Opal Louis Nations

Cover photograph: Sensational Nightingales, 1954-55 – Clockwise from top left:
Bill Woodruff, Carl Coates, John Jefferson, Ernest James, Julius Cheeks
– courtesy Opal Louis Nations.

Cover and book design: Norman Conquest

Scat Trax is an imprint of Black Scat Books
www.BlackScatBooks.com

Black Scat Books
A Scat Trax Edition
BlackScatBooks.com

Other Black Scat Books by Opal Louis Nations

The Complete Unabridged Lexicon

Embryo World & Others Stripped Bare

TABLE OF CONTENTS

Acknowledgements / How the Book Came Together

Over recent years friends have asked "why don't you write a book about your lifelong passion, gospel music?" My immediate thought was, "God, all that work!" I would tire before I got to the end of it. But I came around and thought "what the heck, let's do it." Some four or five years ago I asked Jo Jo Wallace, the last surviving member of the second Sensational Nightingales group, if I might have a crack at writing a book about his life on the gospel highways and byways. He has been out there on the road now with the 'Gales for more than sixty-five years and has many tales to tell.

The thought of handling all this information was at first overwhelming but then I said to myself "he might get someone else to do it, if at all." Much to my surprise, he came through and started sending photographs, pieces of undated information plus various sheets of paper of all shapes and sizes filled to the edges with handwritten remembrances of his childhood and youth.

In spreading out these fragments my immediate thoughts centered on Kurosawa's 1962 classic crime drama, "High and Low" wherein after a kidnapping a team of detectives are given an assortment of clues and the whole puzzle comes together on a huge wall display as gradually information trickles in. All I initially had to go on with my project at first were Jo Jo's fragments, but then Jerry Zolten offered to help and allowed that I use quotes from his book on the Dixie Hummingbirds.

I then contacted my friend Linwood Heath at WNAT in Philadelphia and he supplied me with information gathered from various conversations with Jo Jo plus an interview he conducted with him in recent times. I was able to add all this to photos and factual data from Jo Jo's niece, Annie Gilbert. Working with information I already had, I pieced together what I thought was an interesting book about a top tier quartet whose history needs to be written.

An Introduction: Getting Involved with Writing a Book on the Sensational Nightingales

The question most frequently asked is how did you, an Englishman growing up during the Post-War era in the coastal town of Brighton, ever get so firmly involved in the golden age era of African American gospel quartet music? Well, the short answer is if you track back the spiritual thread of all black American vernacular musics, you inevitably end up outside the church door. With traditional blues, fundamental jazz, developmental R&B and certainly with the awakening of soul balladry, you will often feel (if you are as sensitive about all this as I am) the exquisiteness of a human cry felt at first by ancestral black slaves who had fought hard and long for some semblance of equality.

This very sweet essence of soul can be most strikingly felt in the voices of the gospel singers. By this I am not denying that the same anointing ingredient did not pass through the folk musics of most other worldly societies because by varied cultural means it surely does. Black singers from West Africa and the Caribbean are to my ears the closest spiritual relatives. This begs the second question: "where did you first hear this music and how did your passion for it grow?"

For the most part only the church music of Paul Robeson, Mahalia Jackson and Sister Rosetta Tharpe ever occasionally enjoyed air time over the BBC airwaves. This was despite the fact that two of the three made infrequent visits to the British shores during the Fifties. Little was seen or heard except on old albums found in the shabby-looking pawnshops, places where African American service-men on leave sold their records to finance a night out on the town. Unqualified jazz music columnists always reviewed the odd gospel release in the trade papers. But that was about the sum of it.

It was my good fortune to grow up on the Sussex coast where just a few miles across the English Channel a more refined and certainly more receptive culture prevailed. This was the French.

At times my friends and I rented a beach chalet where we would hold party gatherings on the weekends in order to impress as well as cement relationships with the opposite sex (sadly the latter rarely came about.) But we did take our transistor radios to supply music and augment the booze. On late Sunday nights we tuned into France One where Daniel Filipacchi's weekly American blues and gospel program came on, a one-of-a-kind broadcast. It was on this show during the close of the Fifties we caught the awe-inspiring sounds of the Dixie Hummingbirds, Gospel Clefs, Raymond Rasberry Singers, North Philadelphia Juniors, Staple Singers, and yes, the Sensational Nightingales featuring the heartaching, soul-shaking pipes of the Reverend Julius Cheeks.

This was a life-changing experience I never thought I would ever forget, and I certainly did not. As before, this raises yet another question: "Well, Opal, you profess not to be a spiritual type and not to believe in a Christian God – how do you square your love of gospel music with that?" In my writings and during my lectures I always tell people you do not have to go to church to dig the music. Oh boy, how often in my life have I said that! The worst of it is that your average blues enthusiast is unable to tolerate gospel as much they would the blues.

If you have been around working black folks or have met the less fortunate in the ghettos you would know that for some the church is by necessity the center of these people's lives. Most black churches organize free food and clothing programs and help find temporary housing for those who wind up penniless out on the street. Now do you think that many of these poor forsaken folks have become Christians because they go to church to show thankfulness? Some might, but others attend church because it is the only place to find people who will most likely care for them when no other place can be found. In the United States we do not always care for those less fortunate than ourselves.

Do I feel sorry for the blues enthusiast who gets all out of whack whenever his or her favorite blues celebrity cuts a gospel album? In all likelihood gospel is a part of his musical experience. If they sat down and absorbed the spirit running through the performance they would realize that the only difference between the porch and the pew was the patter. So where did my friends and I go to find gospel records? Why, Paris, of course where they were sold even at major department stores.

The most important French label supporting this music at that time was the international Disques Vogue label on Villetoneuer in Paris. Vogue put out a broad range of musics but its considerable gospel catalogue showed that it leased recordings from Apollo (Mahalia Jackson), Peacock (Spirit of Memphis, Sensational Nightingales, Bells of Joy, Blind Boys of Mississippi, Dixie Hummingbirds plus a host of lesser luminaries), Aladdin (Soul Stirrers) and Vee Jay (Swan Silvertones, Staple Singers and others.) They issued both 10" and 12" albums, singles and extended play 45s.

The company later on put out a series called Mode Disques which included releases by Little Richard, Sister Rosetta Tharpe, Clara Ward and the Sensational Nightingales whose first Peacock album (Peacock 101) under the general title "Negro Spirituals" constituted Mode Disques 9361. Around 1961-1962, Vogue's British subsidiary on London's Fulham Road issued a various artists Peacock album (Vogue LAE 12033) which included many of the above-mentioned quartets plus the Reverend Cleophus Robinson with the Spirit of Memphis, and Christian Travelers.

All of a sudden the gospel collectors' market in Great Britain grew from about ten souls to a count in the three figure range. Unbelievable! English Vogue even started putting out extended play 45s and singles. The ball slowly but cautiously started to roll. Not that it ever gained much momentum. Soon thereafter Columbia Records issued an almost facsimile copy of Vee Jay LP 5016, "Sunday Morning," which introduced us to the extraordinary talents of the Harmonizing Four and Highway Q.C.s. Not stopping here, they later added a beautifully remastered edition of the Stars of Glory, a quartet from OKeh Records.

All of this seemed to be getting out of hand. I began to have dreams of most of South-East England becoming awash in an ocean of gospel music. Soon Fontana Records stepped up to the plate by spewing out a short album series under the banner "Gospel Train" featuring one-offs by the Staple Singers, Patterson Singers, Caravans, Harmonizing Four and the Greater Harvest Baptist Church Choir.

Then just as fast as it had begun everything kind of fell back to a trickle. We were back to a leaky washer with Rosetta and Mahalia's occasional releases. But by then the handful of us who could afford importation started buying from the global mail order guys: Stan's in Shreveport and Ernie's in Nashville. Their prices were fair and reasonable and service was speedy. There ends the short and brief saga of the first Afro-American Post-War Christian soldiers' infiltration.

The gospel collector had to wait for many years before the situation improved somewhat with the growth of the indie label wunderkind, the coming of Charly and Ace Records and the beginning of the reissue movement. I fled England in 1973 wishing to be closer to the sources of my passion and managed to catch most of the fun by finding work in the music business.

Colored Waiting Room, Durham, NC, 1940s – courtesy Opal Louis Nations

A Brief History of Black Gospel Quartet Music in the U.S.

Most folks growing up in the Western world during the 1950s and 1960s have at least come across the most popular African American vocal groups from the 1940s and 1950s such as the Mills Brothers, Ink Spots and Delta Rhythm Boys, the last having appeared in fifteen films during that time. Most would have encountered white pop groups such as the Andrews Sisters, Boswells and Modernaires. But the less celebrated standout black groups of the Forties such as the Charioteers, Four Tunes, Four Knights, Four Vaga-bonds and Jubalaires are just about forgotten by most folk today.

It is said that not one in a hundred thousand people under the age of fifty will have heard of the great gospel pioneers such as the Norfolk Jubilees who recorded for OKeh Records in 1921 and the groundbreaking Golden Gate Quartet or the Bronzemen, to name but a few. There are currently key research bibliographies available, for example Thomas L. Morgan and William Barlow's "From Cakewalks to Concert Halls (1895-1930) [Elliott & Clark, 1992], Jay Warner's "History of American Singing Groups, 1940-1990 [De Capo, 2000], and Doug Seroff's extensive work in the field of black vocal groups in books too numerous to mention.

There has been black vocal group music in Ameri-can for as long as the country imported slaves. The roots of black American folk music begin with the lucky survivors from the slave ships who took their old songs to the cotton fields and corn rows. As time passed the Euro-American styles of singing and rhythm patterns seeped in to African-based musical arrangements. These tunes became the worry-songs and spirituals of the plantations and settlements. They provided the vehicle by which to capture the aural history of African-American lives. White groups like the Virginia Minstrels all painted up in black-face sung "Negro Melodies" and enacted shuffle dances. This kind of parody carried over into the black minstrel tradition. Black singing also spread through the black Baptist churches during the 1840s increasingly so because gatherings in the street were often forbidden. Documentation of quartets heard singing in the fields date back to 1851. Black touring minstrel companies sprang up after the Civil War. Some journeyed as far as Europe as did the Fisk Jubilee Singers in 1875. Cake-walking became popular in the 1880s and 1890s and the traveling quartets in the minstrel shows crossed over to vaudeville, the precursor of the variety show.

Most early groups sang spirituals as well as popular songs and played instruments. The first black quartet to record was the Unique Quartet in 1893. They were characterized as a "negro folk group." Quartet singing crossed into ragtime and through ragtime into coon-songs or coon shouting. From ragtime emerged jass or jazz and from coon shouting came barbershop. The first major black gospel singing group to record was the Dinwiddie Colored Quartet. They recorded two sessions for Monarch (RCA Victor) in October 1902.

Black gospel group recordings covering the 1910 to 1920 period seemed to mostly emanate from church-spirituals. In 1912 the Apollo Jubilee Quartet recorded "Swing low sweet chariot" in a cappella for Columbia Records. The first significant post-Great War gospel quartet was the Four Harmony Kings who recorded extensively while on tour in England during the 1920s. English people at that time seemed to be able to stomach black church music. Maybe this was because the acts presented themselves as a clowning around kind of entertainment, not to be taken too seriously.

The aforementioned Mills Brothers were already singing on the church circuit during the Twenties. The family came through the barbershop tradition and by the late Twenties were enjoying radio exposure. The Mills Brothers were a strong influence over the Ink Spots who came together in 1934 in Indianapolis. Although the Mills Brothers arose from a gospel childhood, they did not think of seriously recording gospel music until 1950. The Ink Spots' first stab at gospel was a 1941 parody entitled "Shout sister shout."

Regionalized jubilee quartet singing flourished in the 1920s. For just a few examples, I include the Golden Echoes out of Nashville, the Rust College and Bethel Quartets out of Memphis, the Monarch Jubilees out of Norfolk, Virginia, the Richmond Starlights and Old South Quartet out of Richmond, Virginia, the Thankful Quartet from Atlanta, the Silver Leaf, Elkins-Payne and Paramount Jubilees out of New York, the Bessemer Sunsets and Birmingham Jubilees from Alabama and the Sunset Four and Pace Jubilees out of Chicago, just to name a few popular outfits.

All of these aforementioned quartets sang in the four, five and six-part harmonic style labeled "jubilee" which was musically akin to hymn singing. Well mannered, rigidly trained, impeccably attired gospel soldiers traveled the hard road, often at the mercy of their church's governing sponsors who fed and housed them. Meanwhile, one of the key figures behind secularization of gospel songs, Professor Thomas Andrew Dorsey, was working to push praise singing out of the rigid context of the formal worship service into the contemporary mainstream prevalent during the latter half of the Twenties.

This was an exhilarating period filled with musical upheaval, exciting for the younger church singer and composer. Dorsey took the simple blues refrain and adapted it for use in the church. Dorsey wrote, published, performed, demonstrated and encouraged this fresh and stimulating art form knowing that if he prevailed the church would eventually come around to seeing things his way.

At first, Dorsey was frowned on by the more conservative elders of the church establishment, but as this new music took hold it came to be known as the new "gospel" music. In the early Thirties Dorsey formed the first significant mixed gender gospel singing group. This outfit traveled far and wide spreading the new gospel wherever people wanted to listen to it. This pioneering group was called the Roberta Martin Singers out of Chicago.

The Thirties saw the coming and conquering of the influential Golden Gate Quartet whose first recordings were made in a small room at the Pope Hotel in Charlotte, North Carolina. The Gates recorded extensively throughout the Thirties for RCA-Bluebird. Members included "Bill" Johnson, baritone, Henry Owens, first tenor, Bill "Highpockets" Langford, second tenor, and Orlandus "Dad" Wilson on bass. All four came out of Booker T. Washington High in Norfolk, Virginia.

In 1936 they started broadcasting over WIS in Columbia, South Carolina. The aggregation graduated to broadcasting five days a week on a morning program. Their popularity spread like wildfire throughout the Carolinas and surrounding states. Impressive sales of their records got them onto NBC and their show was broadcast from coast to coast. The result of this was that young, aspiring gospel singers set up "Gates" sounding jubilee quarters all over the country. The Gates were the nation's strongest influence over the growth of the jubilee gospel quartet phenomenon simply because of their nationwide footprint.

Tiring of the ways blacks were treated in the United States, the Gates moved to Paris, France in 1955. The outfit at that time was made up of one original member, Orlandus Wilson plus Clyde Wright, second tenor, Clyde Riddick, first tenor, and Frank Todd, baritone. The group established a home base in Paris with membership changes taking place over the years. They continued to record in Paris for many years and have never lost their influence over surviving black gospel quartets in the jubilee style.

Gospel quartet singing went through many dramatic changes during its golden decade, 1945 to 1962. During the emergence of rhythm & blues music in the early Fifties, a tougher, more uninhibited approach to gospel singing came moving in. This dramatic, sometimes exhibitionistic show of extrovert redemption was pioneered by lead-singing shouters such as Archie Brownlee of the Blind Boys of Mississippi, Clarence Fountain of the Blind Boys of Alabama, Dewey Young and Solomon Womack with the Swan Silvertones, Jet Bledsoe of the Spirit of Memphis, and of course the Reverend Julius Cheeks with the Sensational Nightingales.

On the distaff side were shout groups like Ruth Davis and the Davis Sisters, Shirley Caesar and Inez Andrews with the Caravans, Ernestine Rundless of the Meditation Singers plus the awesome raggedy pipes of Dorothy Love Coates and the Gospel Harmonettes.

Crooning and the one-mike huddle of standing on a dime, the performance mode of jubilee singing, was being replaced by the jazzier, booming basso, call and response, alternating pitch, falsetto flight, swing lead face-off, microphone throwing, knee drops, thigh slaps, lavish vocal ornamentation, devilish shrieking, dramatic creeps among the assembled and fainting members of the audience "falling out." All the groups were making an effort to perfect the art of absolute ecstasy, an exquisiteness reached by a few. The Soul Stirrers called this pop-off point reaching "sister fluke." Female Pentecostal congregants often broke into holiness dances followed by fits and falling in a helpless state.

Singers such as Nappy Brown, James Brown, Wilson Pickett and Bobby Womack carried this sanctified bag-of-tricks over into the popular music form. All this dramatic flamboyance was matched with physical attire. Groups and soloists outfitted themselves in outlandish colored tuxedos and fancy silk robes. Some churchgoers called it a circus. The younger female fan worshipped the younger slick and dapper quartet lead as one would an adored R&B hero. When Sam Cooke appeared with the Soul Stirrers, the teenage girls sat in the front rows. Competition grew tougher and tougher. Groups ran themselves ragged trying to outdo each other. All wanted to be kings of the road but a good deal of the glitz and glamour hid the fact that most traveling troubadours lived a hand to mouth existence returning home to the beleaguered wife with only one thin dime in your pocket.

Thanks to ministers such as the Reverend James Cleveland and the national choir movement, Reverend Lawrence Roberts, the Banks Brothers and others, gospel music was returned to the sanctuary of the church in the early Seventies. Quartets and small groups began to lose ground. The church became more a means of day to day support for followers of Christ. Touring vocal quartet groups survived but their numbers diminished as the spread of gospel music became more and more expensive and impractical. The price of car maintenance and accommodation outpaced remuneration. It became more a fantasy to follow the romantic road of the gospel vagabond. Choirs with strong ties to local communities became increasingly popular with regular folk trying to make ends meet.

MAIN STREET, WILLIAMSTON, NORTH CAROLINA

Courtesy Opal Louis Nations

All this led to today's mass choir movement, black pride and self reliance and the drawing in of influences from a variety of African American commercial trends. The result of this was the emergence of urban and contemporary gospel, rap and hip hop, gansta-gospel, gospel praise and worship, participatory gospel and genres compartmentalized as contemporary Christian, inspirational and new traditional, all embracing today's state of the art equipment and new studio techniques.

One has to look a little harder but today through the crutch of the Internet you can still find quartets who by some design still stay with a semblance of traditional gospel harmony. Suggested quartets to look for in this vein are Lee Williams and the Spiritual QC's, Willie Rogers and his quartet, and, as always, the Sensational Nightingales who never fail to bring back the good old days of the quartet tradition.

Some of Jo Jo Wallace's Earliest Recollections

Joseph "Jo Jo" Henry Wallace was born in a "shake"-shack on Duddle Hill on October 4th, 1926. His parents, John and Annie B. Wallace, were farming folk on the bare grass settlement (now designated a historic district) on the outskirts back in the woods of Williamston, Martin County, North-East in North Carolina. There were no roads or sidewalks on Duddle Hill and the shake had shutters for windows and a tin roof.

Besides tobacco growing and the presence of lumber companies, Williamston was a peanut growing, cleaning and shelling town which, without federal intervention, would not have survived the Great Depression. In 1943 a prison camp of German and Italian prisoners of war was built near the Roanoke River which floated the area's commercial shipments from Roanoke to Plymouth. The prison camp housed captured soldiers from Rommel's elite Desert Corps. The camp's inmates labored at the Standard Fertilizer Company mill which supported the growth of local farms at critical times.

Jo Jo's earliest memories date back to the time of the stock market crash of October 1929. "I remember mama used to make hoe-cakes and cooking them under the ashes of our old wood stove. I can also recall my grand-daddy always chopping wood and singing some of the old slavery songs, especially the old folk song about John Henry, the steel-driving man. I used to walk down the path to Aunt Maggie's house to draw water from her well in the dirt yard, but it was not very long before we moved down closer to town on Church Street."

As far as I can gather, Jo Jo's father, John Wallace Snr., was born around 1896, at the time of the Klondike gold rush. His wife, Annie Belle Brown-Wallace, was born in 1901 during the time when plans were born to build the Panama Canal. Annie Belle worked most of her young life looking after the domestic needs of surrounding white folk (Jo Jo later helped her out with financial support – she died after the assassination of Martin Luther King Jnr. in Memphis in 1968.)

"I remember my mama taking me to church and sitting me on her knee. I'd listen to the congregation sing those beautiful old hymns that I grew to like so much. Mama prayed for the welfare of the family. Believe it or not, as young as I was, I can recall mama and daddy had an old pump organ given to us by a white family. It had side flaps you could open with your knees. The side flaps enabled an increase in volume when pumping the foot paddles. Mama would sit and play those beautiful old hymns and the words and music would really touch my heart. Those beautiful memories have stayed with me all my life.

During mama's playing my older brother Gus (now sadly deceased) would pick up the bass vocal part from the bass key while my oldest brother, Johnny (John Junior) would catch the appropriate notes given out by the baritone key. At the same time almost by instinct I was soon able to pick out the tenor. We rehearsed these parts until we were able to sing those beautiful hymns in perfect harmony. I have been asked many times the question where did you learn to sing tenor and I tell them I learned by picking up the scales of mama's organ by ear."

Jo Jo tells in another interview that the Wallace clan attended the River Hill Baptist Church, although on occasion Annie Belle took Jo Jo to the Beargrass Baptist in

Upper Winston and set him down in the amen corner. Jo Jo also relates that Gus (Augusta) and mama sang gospel duets around the organ and that John Junior joined in later on. Jo Jo made up the singing quartet when he was old enough to do so. In an interview with Linwood Heath, Jo Jo said he also learned to play a little piano but never made the effort to study how to read music.

Jo Jo's father died around the time the Empire State Building opened in New York City. "When my daddy died mama was sick in hospital suffering from some minor ailment. When the family went to see mama in hospital we were told not to tell her about daddy having passed away in case it worsened her condition. When we all got to the hospital in Little Rock we were looking so sad around the bedside we could sense that mama knew something was wrong. Daddy's body back at the house lay in a cheap casket in the hallway. Mama pulled me over to her side and asked, 'son, where's your daddy?' Well, being just a child and out of respect for mama I told her in a soft voice that daddy was dead. The family looked shocked but mama didn't seem too surprised. I don't think my parents got along that well."

"I remember mama sending me to Walter Mazell's candy store to buy me a Baby Ruth for helping her with washing the clothes. My job was to pump the water into tin tubs. I recall there were three tubs, the first for the washed clothes, the second for the bluing water and the third for the rinse. Sister "Minnie" Margaret and brother Gus helped me peg out the laundry. I'll never forget mama's ironing board – it was just an unfinished cedar-wood plank mama draped the clothes over.

I remember another errand mama sent me out on to buy kerosene with the last ten cents we had. We needed it for the fire in the heater and the lamps. 'Take this gallon jug to the store,' said mama and be careful at the corner when you pass the fire plug. If you get too close, you might bust the jug.' I walked down the path and passed the hydrant. On the way home, feeling happy as I did what mama told me, singing and humming along, I got so distracted that I forgot the hydrant and broke the jug. I stood shaking and trembling 'cause I knew what was to come. Mama took me by my raggedy shirt collar and dragged me up to the back door. 'Stay right there!' she shouted, as I stood shaking with fear. It was not the first time I had watched mama march to the peach tree and break off a switch. Her rule was spare the rod and spoil the child. This time mama wouldn't quit whippin' and in self defense I squeezed my head through between her legs and squeezed them together, but the harder I screamed the worse the beating.

Times were so hard, I'm sure mama tried to take out her trials and tribulations on me. At one point, she did house cleaning for a white lady.

As time passed, my older sister "Minnie" now almost a teenager dated a man named Lightnin' (now deceased) who worked at a printing shop downtown. My brother Johnny worked as a messenger for Western Union and delivered messages by bicycle. He would ride to Lightnin's print shop to borrow his guitar to practice chords on. This was a huge hollow-body model which he'd ride home with. Johnny tried his best to make the chords he had heard mama play on the pump organ. After a struggle he came to a point where he could make just three chords. I'd sit between his legs on the floor looking at his left hand trying to figure out his moves. He would make the same chords every sitting. When it came time for him to go to work he placed the instrument in the corner of the house. He would shout: 'you better not mess with that guitar!'

I was scared but when he left the house and rode out of sight I'd run and pick up the guitar which was almost as large as I was. I tried to pick out the chords he had made as best I remembered them. Problem was I could hardly reach my arms around the instrument to hold it but I was determined. Somehow I managed to remember all I had learned listening to mama play the old hymns and could transcribe the chords to the guitar. Mama heard me play and was taken by surprise. She had my brother John Junior sit and listen. I knew that if the order came from her, I wouldn't be punished for using the instrument. But when I ran excitedly to fetch the guitar, brother Johnny tried to stop me, but mama over-ruled his objection. Johnny was at first surprised and then jealous of my skill. He never borrowed Lightnin's guitar after that."

"So when "Minnie" went out on a date, she asked to borrow Lightnin's guitar on my behalf. I practiced whenever I could after that. I even took it to bed with me. Johnny got his revenge later on though. One day Johnny offered to take me to town. He took my hand to make me feel secure and off we went. Halfway down the block Johnny decided to cross the street. Cars were running left and right. Johnny looked in both directions and couldn't see any cars coming. 'Okay!' he shouted, 'Go ahead.' I started out crossing as fast as I could. Then, seeing a car coming, he shouted "Come back!' I jumped back quickly. He grabbed my hand and said, 'Next time I'll tell you when to go.'"

"Just at that time a car was coming around the curve and Johnny didn't see it. 'Okay, go ahead,' he said. I trusted him and took off. Then he shouted again, 'Come back, come back!' Well, by then I was halfway across the street but thought I could make it. Unfortunately, the car kept on going so I rushed on back and by a stroke of luck I made it safely. Then we tried to cross a third time. After all, I trusted Johnny to get me safely across. I was halfway when Johnny shouted 'Come back, come back!' I thought this time I could make it. It was a Saturday evening and it looked like the driver and his pals had had a little too much to drink. They were out having fun and were driving way too fast. Being no taller than the distance of the headlight from the ground my face hit the light fair and square and the impact knocked me four feet into the air."

"Luckily I landed on the soft grass meridian between the sidewalk and the highway. I remember lying face down with one eye hanging out and Johnny calling 'Jo, is you hurt, is you hurt?' Johnny picked me up and we headed for home. Along the way we ran into daddy and he took me in his arms and rushed me to the only doctor us black folk had in town, a doctor Rose. After treatment, the doctor bandaged up my head so that only my good eye was left showing. He also cut an air passage across my mouth just big enough to pass a straw. At one point the doctor thought I'd lose sight in one eye." Jo Jo's recovery was spent in a crib.

Because Jo Jo is a very kind and giving person, he so often covers up the shortcomings of those he cares about the most. This seems to be the case with the last story. He is known to tell it a different way. This second version we must assume took place after his father's death. "One Saturday night when I was around six and a half years old my brother and I took a trip to town down River Hill. I always liked riding on Johnny's shoulders so I was pretty happy doing so that night. When we had gone some distance, a bunch of rowdy drunks came lurching around the corner in our direction. Johnny set me down and ran off. Being an innocent child, not thinking I was in any danger, I walked on. The rowdies grabbed me and punched me repeatedly in the head. Some of my teeth were broken. They punched me so hard that I flew into the air a few times. My face grew swollen and was covered in blood. I was found later lying motionless on the ground. The family thought I'd never pull through. Congealed lumps of blood were taken from inside my mouth and a straw was inserted so that I could breathe more easily." Whether this is a different story or not is anybody's guess, but both make good copy.

"Apart from being beaten by a bread truck driver for dropping a box of bread, I wore my mama's homemade peach tree switch down to a nub." Between times Johnny and Jo Jo attended Williamston's grade school where both got into more scrapes.

Jo Jo's Father's Death and the Move to Philadelphia

Some of Jo Jo's early recollections are strange and mysterious. It is strange that he knew only by name the existence of his oldest brother, Buck. He had neither seen him or had any dealings with him. While Jo Jo and his older siblings worked in the cotton fields (Jo Jo brags he could pick two rows at once) and tobacco plantations up on River Hill, his mother worked her fingers to the bone catering to white folk by cleaning and pressing their laundry for four dollars a bundle. Jo Jo's father meanwhile worked as a truck driver. He ran his own trucking company with two of his friends. Each had their own truck. The three drove in convoy from Williamston North to the sandpits just outside Windsor. They would load up with sand and return to Williamston. The work was dangerous. Loaders died when sand-holes collapsed in bad weather.

Jo Jo's father's untimely death was reported in the local papers as being the result of an unfortunate accident. He was found dead fully clothed in a sand-hole along with his two fully dressed partners. A group of white boys was seen in the area but no evidence of foul play ever came to light. It was the early Thirties and black folk in the Carolinas like those in the Deep South lived marginal lives as second class citizens.

John Junior, second oldest son, was born around 1919. He served in the military during the War and later became a certified electrician. After a gospel singing spell, he became a Church of God in Christ minister. John Junior and Jo Jo were inseparable pals during childhood. John passed in 2006. Next down in age was "Minnie" Margaret Wallace born in 1922. Her profession was simply noted as a "packer." What this entails is not known. She died in 1971. Next down in age was Augusta "Gus" Wallace, born in 1924. He lived until age 57. Little is known about him also. Jo Jo was the last born. Inez Evelyn Jones Wallace, Jo Jo's wife, was born in Fayetteville, North Carolina, the second of eleven children. She married Jo Jo in August 1964. She preferred to stay in the background, never wanting to interfere with Jo Jo's ministry. She passed in August 2009.

When Jo Jo was eight or perhaps nine years old, his mama took a Greyhound bus trip to Philadelphia to stay with an aunt for a while. She had met a man (a Mr. Burns) and they married soon after Jo Jo's arrival in the city. They had one daughter, Vera. As with many other aforementioned family members, information about Vera is scant.

After mama's departure to Philadelphia Jo Jo wrote and told her how much he missed her. "Mama made an arrangement for me to come see her," said Jo Jo. "When I got to the Wiliamston bus depot the bus company pinned a travel aid tag to my jacket. Being a green country boy I'd never seen anything except squirrels and rabbits and rolling hills. Imagine my amazement when I saw skyscrapers and huge buildings along the highways. It was like a scene from King Kong. Being ignorant of the outside world and in particular city life, when I reached Philadelphia I fell in with a bad crowd. As a teen I got myself into a lot of trouble. I made many bad mistakes. These things were talked about and mama got riled up to a point when she had to act real tough with me. I realized I was bringing hardship to others. That made me think about cleaning myself up. Out of concern for mama I went out and found a regular job. We needed the extra cash real bad so I started out as a spray finisher at the Gill Fixture Company. It was my job to hand spray finish on strip lights." According to Jo Jo's niece, Annie Gilbert, this was the only 9-to-5 job Jo Jo ever filled.

The Philadelphia Gospel Scene in the mid-20th Century

Today, gospel quartet singing coming out of Philadelphia is best remembered through the female quartets with the likes the Clara and Gertrude Ward Singers, Davis Sisters, Angelic Gospel Singers and other female squads usually accompanied by a pianist. Equally talented female groups, like the Gospel Descendents, remain overlooked. Others remember the importance of composer / pioneer Charles Albert Tindley (1851-1933), author of the gospel primer "Gospel Pearls," founder of the Tindley Gospel Singers, and writer of such classic gospel hymns as "The Lord will make a way" and "We'll understand it better by and by." Tindley, as minister of the Tindley Temple, often opened his church to performances by local gospel aggregations, both amateur and professional.

Philadelphia's Convention Hall also provided a large performance space for gospel singers as did The Met with programs hosted by Louise Williams and Bonnie Dee. On a smaller scale, Baptist churches like the Ebenezer, Pilgrims' Rest C.O.G.I.C., Zion Apostolic Temple and concert halls such as the Uptown Theatre staged concerts. Two principal indie record companies issued gospel recordings. These were Gotham on Ninth Avenue, founded by Ivin Ballen and retail mogul Sam Goode in 1947, and Grand on Lancaster Avenue, proprietored by Herb Slotkin founded in 1953. Both recorded in a sparse way a few of the gospel talents the city had to offer. Gotham recorded the Norfolk Four, Angelic Gospel Singers, Dixie Hummingbirds, Davis Sisters, Clara Ward and among others, the Silveraires in which Jo Jo and his brother John Junior had served (more about them a little later.)

Grand did not record much local gospel talent but according to gospel researcher Linwood J. Heath, they opened up their basement, the Treegoob's Record Store space to local and visiting gospel talents to perform. Heath remembers a great number of Philly groups, singers with tremendous skills like the Capitol City Stars who recorded for Revelation in Harlem, Gate City Singers on Apollo, the under-recorded Bay State Singers, Welcome Travelers, Silver Crowns with Deacon Green, Williams Brothers, and the Sacred Harmonizers, also on Revelation. All are today fondly recalled by the older fans among us.

Willa Ward-Royster remembers the versatile Eureka Glee Chorus for whom she played piano. Her sister, Clara Ward, also tickled the ivories for the North Carolina Jubilee Quartet of whom the great Paul Owens was a member. Both Owens and Ira Tucker of the Dixie Hummingbirds taught gospel singing to amateurs at rehearsals all over the city. Linwood J. Heath relates that long-serving Dixie Hummingbird guitarist Howard Carroll remembers seeing aspiring gospel singers / songwriters walking Philadelphia neighborhoods and standing on street corners every Saturday, all the while singing songs they had composed and selling the lyric sheets to them for 10 cents a pop. No matter that music notes had not been written out -- buyers would simply recall the singers' renditions later on.

Jo Jo and John Junior's Early Philadelphia Days plus the Silveraires

In the late 1930s, Jo Jo and John Junior made a regular habit of tuning in to the Golden Gate Quartet's radio broadcasts over powerful WBT in Charlotte. The Gates closely sang spirituals, inspired many a singer, including Jo Jo and John Junior. They wanted to establish a jubilee quartet and sound just like them. They were also inspired by the pioneering Selah Quartet, led by singer / manager / disc jockey Thurman Ruth who later presented gospel music caravans (programs) at Harlem's Apollo Theatre. The Selahs enjoyed a radio show over WPTF in Raleigh, North Carolina. The station was a 50,000 megawatt facility that blanketed many states. One of the Selah's original tenors was Reverend Nathaniel Townsley who was partly responsible for launching the original Nightingales' career.

After John Junior got out of the Service he and Jo Jo joined a local Philadelphia church group called the Heavenly Gospel Singers (this was not the celebrated Heavenly Gospel Singers on Manor Records.) It was here that Jo Jo honed his skills as a guitar accompanist. It was not long before John and Jo Jo quit the Heavenlys and hitched up with the Silveraires out of Wilmington, North Carolina. The Silveraires were founded by bass singer John McLaurin and baritone John Evans. The Silveraires added tenors John Junior and Jo Jo with Jo Jo doubling on guitar accompaniment. Lead singer during this time was Haizo Miles of whom little is known.

All the guys worked day jobs and rehearsed during the evenings at the Wallace house which was by now filled with most of Jo Jo's siblings from North Carolina. Soon the

Silveraires became popular around The City of Brotherly Love. They started appearing on programs in towns and cities a weekend's drive away. The Silveraires always turned out impeccably dressed, sometimes in grey or rented navy blue tuxedos, and sometimes in regular suits with matching ties and patent leather shoes. In no time at all they were hosting a regular twenty-minute radio show over Philadelphia's WCAU. They were introduced as "And now the voices of the Silveraires!" And after this announcement, the quartet would go into their opening theme song, "I heard the heavenly bells ringing" which Jo Jo asserts they lifted from the Golden Gate Quartet. I have been unable to trace any song by this title recorded by the Golden Gate Quartet so we must conclude that it would have been sung by them only in live concerts or over the radio.

You might think that throughout the Post-War period Philadelphia would be jumping with indie record labels but that was not the case. As John Broven says, "Philadelphia was too much in the shadow of New York" to have a vibrant recording scene of their own. All this was before the onslaught of the teeny bopper American Bandstand phenomenon. Grand Records had a strong presence but did not support much gospel music. Gotham Records was really the only game in town. They had signed major gospel talent like the Norfolk Four and the ground-breaking Blue Jay Singers from out of town. All this changed when the Dixie Hummingbirds signed with the label in July 1949, six months after the Silveraires' signing in January.

The Silveraires were a perfect match when opening programs for the Dixie Hummingbirds. Gotham also took care of the Silveraires' booking and management under the Gotham Attractions header. The Silveraires were then slated to appear with Baltimore's own CBS Trumpeteers when the latter were still riding high with their hit recording "Milky White Way." This was major exposure for the Silveraires. As a result of this the group cut seven singles for Gotham between January 1949 and October 1950. The most impressive included the beautifully balanced harmonies on W.B. Stevens' "Farther along" done in the jubilee style, Edna Gallmon Cooke's soulful "In my heavenly home" and the Gates-like flavoring of "End of my journey." The group's touching hymn-empowered reading of "Shine on me" is equally well perfected as any version I have ever heard.

The Silveraires sang "sweet" and in keeping with the conventional quartet tradition. The Silveraires' version of Fanny Crosby's "Near the cross" was used by local gospel deejay John Crain as his theme. Sadly, the jubilee style was fading out of fashion in favor of a more extrovert expression of gospel. If jubilee singing had prevailed their fortunes might have increased. However, the Silveraires traveled throughout the Carolinas and at one point played in Jo Jo's home town of Williamston. The Silveraires split up somewhere near the close of 1950.

The Original Nightingales ('Gales)

According to Howard Carroll (born Philadelphia April 27, 1925), the history of the 'Gales dates back to just after World War II with an outfit formed in Philadelphia Carroll remembers as the Lamplighters. Soldiers included Jerome Guy, tenor, Sam Whitley, bass, Junior Overton, lead, and Theodore Price, baritone. Although the Lamplighters were primarily a gospel-singing group, they also embraced jazz, blues and the popular songs of the day in their repertoire. Quartets like the Jubileers and Charioteers also built similar comprehensive songbooks, because at some venues it was customary to field a wide variety of requests from the patrons.

This pleased the management and increased the chances of the act finding work in a competitive market. In some cases this expansion lengthened the tenure of the artist's contract.

A quartet called the Landlighters was also working around the area in the late Forties. The Landlighters recorded "I've got a home" backed with "You've got to lean" for Bess Berman's Apollo Records (Apollo 212) in 1949. Could Howard Carroll be referring to the Landlighters who recorded this one gospel single in New York? Carroll states that he played a few shows for the Lamplighters and then formally joined the group in March 1946. Later, in 1949, Guy and Carroll changed the group name to the Nightingale Quartet. Bird groups like the Famous Blue Jays and the Dixie Hummingbirds seemed the order of the day. Deciding to stick solely to gospel singing, the Nightingale

Quartet played concerts around Philadelphia and appeared on a regular radio show broadcast from the St. James Hotel. Overton had a day job that got him off work late. This made it difficult for the group to fulfill out-of-town engagements. Paul James Owens (born July 27th 1924 in Greensboro, North Carolina) was persuaded to join to cover the out-of-town work. Owens had been with several Philadelphia gospel quartets, including the Israelite Gospel Singers and the Bay State Gospel Singers.

The Bay State Singers often opened for the Dixie Hummingbirds who were managed by Barney L. Parks. Owens was not only a widely experienced vocalist, he served as a vocal coach for many aspiring quartet and choral singers. The Nightingale Quartet still suffered a lack of name recognition. They were virtually unknown outside of Philadelphia. It was the Reverend Nathaniel Townsley who (as was mentioned before) sung in the legendary Norfolk Jubilees and tenor with the Selahs with support from Owens that introduced the group to Barney L. Parks (born July 15, 1915 in Wilmington, South Carolina.)

In Greenville, Parks and James Davis formed the nucleus in the late 1920s of what was to become the Dixie Hummingbirds. Parks was raised in a sanctified church, the Bethel Church of God Holiness in Greenville. The church rocked as hard as the holy rollers. The first Dixie Hummingbirds quartet of Greenville in 1928 was made up of James Davis, tenor, his brother-in-law Barney Parks, baritone, Fred Owens, bass, and lead Bonnie Gipson Junior.

Personnel changed over the years as the group gained celebrity. Parks and Davis sang in and managed the group up to the Dixie Hummingbirds' first recordings for Decca in 1939. At that point, Fred Baker sang tenor and Jimmy Bryant sang bass to make up the quartet. Parks was drafted into the Service in 1943, a year before the group moved on to Regis Records with personnel that included Davis plus Beachy Thompson, second tenor, Ira B. Tucker, baritone, and William Bobo, bass, a lineup which lasted through until 1950 when Ernest James joined the group (more about Ernest James later.)

When Parks was discharged from the Service in 1945 he wanted to rejoin the world of gospel quartet. For one reason or another, he chose not to sing but to manage. He certainly had the knowledge and managerial expertise to put the Nightingales on the right track. First he had to re-shuffle membership. Some soldiers had families and could not commit to extensive travel. With a few swap-outs the group ended up composed of Howard Carroll, baritone and guitar, Paul Owens, lead tenor, Ben Joyner, tenor, and basso William Henry who was plucked out of the Dixie Hum-mingbirds. It seems that Parks still had some pull over his former group, despite the intervening absence over the War years.

During a tour that took the 'Gales through New Jersey they caught the ear of Benny Wells and Lander Cole-man of Coleman Records. The pair operated from out of the basement of their Coleman Hotel, owned and operated since 1948 by the Coleman family at 59 Court Street in Newark. Lander with his brothers and cousins namely Rus-sell, Everette, Wallace and Melvin plus Danny Owens used the hotel as a base of operations. They toured frequently as a gospel group in their own right, the Coleman Brothers.

The Colemans' performance highlight was to appear on the CBS Hootenanny Show in March 1947. The Cole-mans were often seen on the same programs with national-ly recognized quartets, many of whom namely the National Clouds of Joy, Five Blind Boys of Mississippi, Matchless

Love Gospel Singers, Harmonizing Four and Five Blind Boys of Alabama not only stayed at the Coleman Hotel but also recorded for the family-owned Coleman record label. This convenient arrangement made it possible for top talent to stay in one place and to work up material which might end up on shellac and be distributed through the Colemans' own distribution network down the East Coast.

If it were not for Lander and Benny, many of the big name, or soon to be big name quartets like the Nightingale Quartet might never have successfully launched their careers.

The Nightingale Quartet cut one session at the Coleman Hotel in June 1949 from which three releases emerged during late 1949 and into 1950. Among the most notable of these were the Paul Owens-led songs "Get away Jordan," "Savior don't pass me by" and "In the room with the Lord." Owens was quite clearly not only the adhesive that held the group together but the driving force that eventually took the group out of stand-on-a-dime jubilee into a more demonstrative technique. All this took time, as we shall see.

Parks put the Nightingale Quartet onto programs headed by Sister Rosetta Tharpe, as he had done with the 'Birds. Parks was a tough task-master who ran the Nightingales as he did the "Birds," like the leader of a military squad. He put the group on radio in Wilson, North Carolina, after rehearsing them relentlessly in nearby Goldsboro. In December 1949, billed simply as the Nightingales, the group recorded one a cappella session for Syd Nathan's King Records at New York's Beltone Studios. Five titles were etched with Owens at the helm. The songs seemed to lack luster and drive and the absence of Howard Carroll's guitar accompaniment did not help much.

Legend has it that Syd Nathan particularly asked that

the group sound 'folksy' to appeal to a broader, white audience. But I doubt this. The song treatments sounded controlled, both in style and arrangement and seemed aurally to pre-date the Coleman sides. It was felt afterwards that something needed to be done to add more voltage to the Nightingale Quartet sound.

The Reverend Julius "June" Cheeks

As writer Jasen Ankeny states, "At the peak of his career during the mid Fifties the Reverend Julius "June" Cheeks was a definitive hard gospel singer famed for his gritty powerhouse baritone and his magical ability to grab and hold his listeners' attention." Cheeks' approach to preacherly singing replicated the stereotypical lil' 'ole country minister who often ended his exhaustive sermon in a state of emotional catharsis. Not only were other gospel leading lights influenced by his "anointing," artists such as the late Robert Blair of the Violinaires, Little Joe Willie Ligon of the Mighty Clouds of Joy and Clarence Fountain of the Blind Boys of Alabama, to name a few, soloists over in the popular music genre such as Wilson Pickett (who was the embodiment of Cheeks), James Brown and Little Richard fell under his spell.

When it boils down to it Cheeks and the legendary Archie Brownlee, one-time tenor lead of the Five Blind Boys of Mississippi, founded the 'saved and sanctified' school of hard-as-rock gospel singing. Brownlee often refused to sing on the same program as Cheeks because if Cheeks hit the footlights first there would not be a saint left standing when he and the Blind Boys came on. Brownlee's work would already be done. He would not have been able to move the house.

Cheeks came up from dire poverty. He was born in Spartanburg, South Carolina on August 7th, 1929. The family was dirt poor sharecroppers. His mother, known to family and friends as 'Big Chick,' was a widow remembered for her tough, stern manner. 'Big Chick's' fierce determination to keep her twelve-strong brood alive rubbed off on 'June' in ways that were seen and felt in his every performance. 'Big Chick' raised as many children as her poor, tired body would allow. More children meant more hands in the cotton-fields. Extra bales picked translated into more meals prepared. Without a steady father around to help out the children were pushed out into the cotton-fields at a tender age. Full education was a privilege the family could not afford.

Because 'June' worked the hardest out in the fields he was kept from schooling after second grade. He had figured out how to sign his own name but never fully learned how to read and write. "We were so poor," said 'June', "we were never able to buy even a clock." This meant that the brood worked and slept by the rising and setting of the sun. The family diet consisted mainly of fatback and molasses. 'June' borrowed from a neighbor a set of 78 RPM recordings that contained readings from the bible. He found another soul with a phonograph and that way listened to the holy scriptures that by learning so well he was able to remember every word of them.

At the age of twelve he graduated from field hand to water boy. He discovered yet another neighbor with a radio and was able to enjoy Sunday morning gospel broadcasts. He took pleasure in listening to the Soul Stirrers and Dixie Hummingbirds over the airwaves. He caught the gospel singing bug and joined a local down-homey group called the Baronets. The Baronets were fortunate enough to sing on a local radio program with Paul Owens and the original Nightingales. Barney L. Parks, then manager of the Nightingales, Edna Gallmon Cook and the Singing Sons, liked what he heard and put 'June' with the Singing Sons who at that point consisted of David Edrington (sometimes spelt

Eddington), lead tenor (Edrington became a Nightingale in the late Fifties), James Brown, tenor (Brown went on to sing in the Selah Singers), Carl Davis, second tenor (Davis sang in the Swan Silvertones many years later) and bass, Providence Thomas (Thomas sang in many quartets but wound up singing with 'June' in the Four [Gospel] Knights in the early Sixties.)

Parks often switched his singers around to meet with booking requirements. Horace Thompson from Gainsville, Florida (who joined the Sensational Nightingales in 1963) also sang tenor in a later configuration of the Singing Sons. Parks had managed to get the Singing Sons under contract with Decca in 1949 and when putting the revitalized second Nightingales group together in 1950, having already established a relationship with Decca, found it easier to have his new Nightingales signed with them.

PHOTO GALLERY

Sensational Nightingales, 1952. Left to right, top: John Jefferson,
Julius Cheeks; Bottom: Bill Woodruff, Ernest James, Jo Jo Wallace
– courtesy Opal Louis Nations

Jordan Brown, Jo Jo Wallace's grandfather – courtesy Annie Gilbert

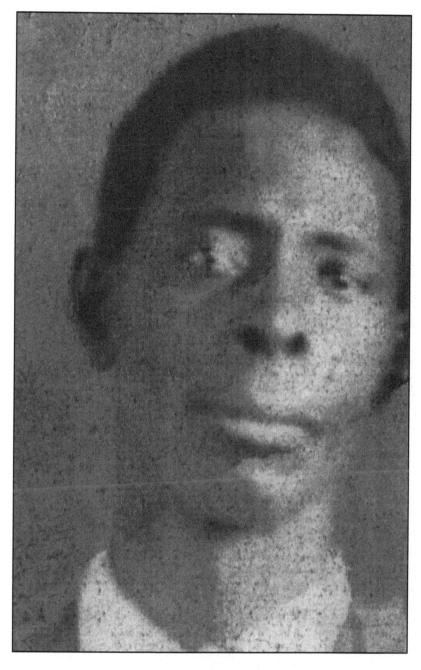

John Wallace, Jo Jo Wallace's father – courtesy Annie Gilbert

Annie Bell Wallace, Jo Jo Wallace's mother – courtesy Jo Jo Wallace

Theodore ("Buck") Wallace – Jo Jo Wallace's oldest brother
– courtesy Annie Gilbert

Jo Jo Wallace and siblings – courtesy Jo Jo Wallace

Jo Jo Wallace, age 13 – courtesy Annie Gilbert

Nightingales (earliest photo, unknown date and personnel)
– courtesy Paul Owens

Sensational Nightingales, 1951 – Back row: Ben Joyner, William Henry,
Howard Carroll; front row: Paul Owens & Julius "June" Cheeks.
- Courtesy Jerry Zolten

REV. JULIUS CHEEKS
Mgr. Sensational Nightingales

Julius Cheeks, late 1950s – courtesy Sherry S. Dupree

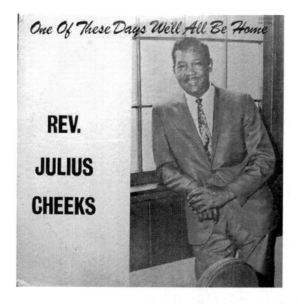

*Julius Cheeks – One of These Days We'll All Be Home album cover
– Su-Ann 1754 (1975) – courtesy Opal Louis Nations*

*Julius Cheeks – Gospel – Disques Pop EP MPO.3105
– courtesy Opal Louis Nations*

The teenage Jo Jo Wallace – courtesy Annie Gilbert

Silveraires with Jo Jo Wallace (guitar), 1949 – courtesy Jo Jo Wallace

Jo Jo Wallace, 2010 – courtesy Jo Jo Wallace

Barney L. Parks (founder of the Sensational Nightingales)
– courtesy Jo Jo Wallace

Sensational Nightingales – Songs of Praise - Peacock LP PLP 101 (1960)
– courtesy Opal Louis Nations

Sensational Nightingales – Negro Spirituals – French version of
Peacock LP PLP 101 – courtesy Opal Louis Nations

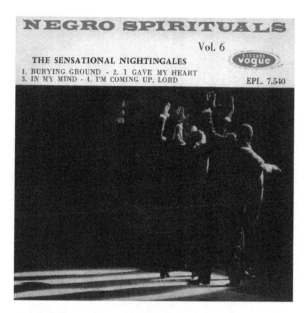

Sensational Nightingales – Negro Spirituals Vol. 6 – Disques Vogues EPL 7540 – courtesy Opal Louis Nations

The late Inez Evelyn Jones Wallace (Jo Jo Wallace's wife) – courtesy Jo Jo Wallace

Five Singing Sons of North, S.C. (later group, 1970s)
– courtesy Opal Louis Nations

Gospel Consolators, 1955 – Charles Johnson, far right – courtesy Opal Louis Nations

Gospel Consolators, 1958-1959 – Charles Johnson, front row, third from the left
– courtesy Opal Louis Nations

Julius Cheeks & The Four Gospel Knights, 1964
– courtesy Opal Louis Nations

Julius Cheeks & The Four Gospel Knights (1964) – TV Gospel Time
– courtesy Fisk University

Charles Johnson & the Revivers, 1984 - Charles Johnson, 2nd from left
- courtesy Charles Johnson

Sensational Nightingales - performance placard - 1984 - courtesy Mark Carrodus

Sensational Nightingales, 1956 – Clockwise from left: Dave Edrington, Bill Woodruff, Jo Jo Wallace, Carl Coates, Julius Cheeks, Herbert Robinson – courtesy Opal Louis Nations

Sensational Nightingales, mid-1950s – Back row, L-to-R: John Jefferson, Bill Woodruff, Jo Jo Wallace; Center: Ernest James; Bottom: Tommy Ellison – courtesy Annie Gilbert

*Sensational Nightingales – Newsclipping, Gary Gazette, Vol. 1, no. 11
(mid-1950s) – "Lucky Cordell's 5th Anniversary Program" – L-to_R: Jo Jo Wallace,
Bill Woodruff, John Jefferson, Ernest James, Tommy Ellison
– courtesy Annie Gilbert*

Sensational Nightingales – Mid-1950s – with tractor – (Jo Jo Wallace & David Edrington with hands raised); Front, L-to-R: Julius Cheeks + unidentified person; far right: John Jefferson – courtesy Annie Gilbert

Sensational Nightingales – Apollo Theatre lobby card, mid-1950s – L-to-R:
John Jefferson, Ernest James, Julius Cheeks (hidden: Bill Woodruff); Far right:
Jo Jo Wallace – courtesy Annie Gilbert

The Reverend Julius "June" Cheeks and the Sensational Nightingales

Sensational Nightingales – Apollo Theater, 1958 – Left-to-right: Carl Coates, Dewey Young, Julius Cheeks, Jo Jo Wallace, Bill Woodruff (hidden behind Cheeks: David Edrington) – courtesy Horace Clarence Boyer

The Sensational Nightingales

Sensational Nightingales – Late 1950s (5 members) – Back row, L-to-R: Julius Cheeks, Jo Jo Wallace & unidentified; Front row: Bill Woodruff, Carl Coates – courtesy Annie Gilbert

Sensational Nightingales – Early 1960s – Back row, L-to-R:
David Edrington & Bill Woodruff; Front row, L-to-R: Jo Jo Wallace & Carl Coates
– courtesy Annie Gilbert

Sensational Nightingales, 1960 – Back row: Bill Woodruff, Jo Jo Wallace; front row: Carl Coates, David Edrington, Herbert Robinson, Ernest James – Courtesy Ray Funk

Sensational Nightingales – Early 1960s snapshot – L-to-R: Bill Woodruff,
David Edrington, Carl Coates, Jo Jo Wallace, Julius Cheeks
– courtesy Annie Gilbert

*Sensational Nightingales – TV Gospel Time, 1964 – L-to-R: Carl Coates,
Bill Woodruff, Charles Johnson, Rudolph Leamon (?), Jo Jo Wallace
– courtesy Fisk University*

Sensational Nightingales, ca. 1966 – Back row, L-to-R: Jo Jo Wallace & Bill Woodruff; Front row, L-to-R: Carl Coates, Charles Johnson, Horace Thompson – courtesy Opal Louis Nations

*Sensational Nightingales – Promo photo, 1967 – Clockwise, L-to-R: Bill
Woodruff, Horace Thompson, Charles Johnson, Jo Jo Wallace
– courtesy Opal Louis Nations*

*Sensational Nightingales – Back cover photo from Peacock LP 175 (1972) – L-to-R:
Horace Thompson, Jo Jo Wallace, Charles B. Johnson, Bill Woodruff
– courtesy Opal Louis Nations*

Sensational Nightingales on stage overseas, 1991 – L-to-R: Calvert McNair, Bill Woodruff, Horace Thompson, Jo Jo Wallace – courtesy Jo Jo Wallace

THE SENSATIONAL NIGHTINGALES   Booking Manager:
BRO. JOSEPH WALLACE
(919) 682-1295

Sensational Nightingales – Promo photo, ca. 1992 – Clockwise from top center: Horace Thompson, Bill Woodruff, Jo Jo Wallace, Calvert Owen McNair – courtesy Jo Jo Wallace

Peacock 1704 – *A soldier not in uniform* (1952)

Peacock 1761 – *Lord have mercy* (1953)
– lead: J. Cheeks & E. James

Peacock 1728 – *I'm going on with Jesus* (1954)
– lead: Ernest James

Peacock 1739 – *Go where Jesus is* (1954)
– lead: James & Cheeks

Peacock 1749 – *Somewhere to lay my head* (1955)
– lead: Cheeks

Peacock 1794 – *A closer walk with Thee* (1959)
– lead: Cheeks

Peacock 1814 – *Who is that* (1959) – lead: Cheeks

Peacock 1826 – *Canaan land* (1960) – lead: H. Robertson

Peacock 1858 – *Blood for me* (1962)

Peacock 1859 – *Holy wine* (1962) – Rev. Julius Cheeks

Peacock 1870 – *Don't put off today* (1962)

Peacock 3070 – *New Jerusalem* (1965)

Peacock 3088 – *Prayed too late* (1965)

All label shots courtesy Opal Louis Nations

The Second Nightingales Group – The Sensational Nightingales

It was in late 1950 that Parks came looking for Julius 'June' Cheeks to head up the newly invigorated Nightingales. This was when Paul Owens and Howard Carroll were still in the group along with Ben Joyner and William Henry. Legend has it that Cheeks was pumping gas at a service station in Spartanburg at the time. Parks gave Cheeks ten dollars and told him to meet him in Charleston that evening. Cheeks was excited and was determined to get there. So began weeks of endless rehearsals which, as it turned out, made Cheeks a professional showman and harmonist.

Through his connections with Decca Parks managed to get the new Nightingales on two Marie Knight sessions in New York. As background singers on the January 1951 session the Nightingales turned out a magnificent job supporting Knight on "On revival day" and "Sending up my timber," although the Singing Sons might have done equally well in their place. On the February 1951 session Paul Owens and Marie Knight shared lead on B.B. McKinney's "Satisfied with Jesus." During a telephone conversation I had with Paul Owens he told me that he remembered this gig as one of his finest moments.

The Nightingales also supported Marie Knight on George Bennard's "Old rugged cross." Later that month (probably due to their first rate performance behind Marie Knight) the Nightingales were given a session to themselves, on which Cheeks sang first or second lead with Paul Owens on four songs. On "My rock" (shared lead) one hears a fairly well mannered, reigned in 'June' Cheeks. On

"There's a vacant room in heaven," a Cheeks solo, and "Live so God can use you" (a shared lead) we experience much the same thing, but on "Our Father," which was led solely by 'June' Cheeks, we hear a more animated performance although it seems that Paul Owens was pretty much calling the shots. All this caused a lot of friction and Howard Carroll got caught in the cross-fire.

After a tour to California both Howard Carroll and Paul Owens called it quits. There were irreconcilable differences between them and Cheeks. The situation turned out fine in the end. Paul Owens was able to join the Dixie Hummingbirds and was swapped with hard-tenor lead Ernest James who was quite a match for Cheeks who found himself competing against a powerful sparring partner. Paul Owens felt more comfortable being in a group whose members were a little more 'predictable.' Howard Carroll joined the Dixie Hummingbirds in 1953 and stayed with the group for many years.

In 1952 the Nightingales became the Sensational Nightingales and began to live up to this soubriquet in every sense of the word. With Cheeks and James at the helm the group really took off. Cheeks' anguished squalling pitted against James' high tenor screams turned the Sensational Nightingales into a force to be reckoned with. As Howard Carroll related to Seamus McGarvey in a 2005 article, "June could come in a church or any place, and I don't care what the (previous) groups had done, he could tear it down. When it come to spirit June was powerful, June would move and what not, but he just had something that nobody else had."

Problems arose when petty rivalries got in the way. Both lead soloists strove to outdo each other. Nevertheless, the Cheeks-James fission-making switch-leads lasted for at least two glorious years, a period when no self-respecting quartet had the moxy to come on after the 'Gales had fired the place up. They earned the label "the baddest quartet on the road." Quartet competition was fierce. Some singers sang themselves so ragged they had to quit the Gospel Highway to seek out rest and medical attention. Some sweat-drenched singers ran madly down the aisles and out of the church door only to collapse and to perish in freezing temperatures outside.

During mid-1952 both Barney L. Parks' groups, the 'Birds and the 'Gales had signed with Don Robey's Peacock Records in Houston. By now Jo Jo Wallace had been hired by Parks to sing both tenor and play guitar for the 'Gales. Cheeks became first lead baritone and James second lead tenor. Baritone Willie George "Bill" Woodruff (born in Spartanburg, South Carolina on January 15, 1929) and basso John Jefferson (born March 30, 1926 in Madison, Georgia) constituted the other members of the group. Woodruff, the son of a bass singer, sang in the Mello-Tones who recorded for Columbia Records before coming to the 'Gales. Parks picked up Woodruff at his flower shop in Spartanburg. Woodruff was eager to join the group. Parks then plucked up Jo Jo Wallace in Philadelphia and John Jefferson in Madison, Georgia.

The Sensational Nightingales enjoyed one long session for Peacock in July 1952. Six songs were put in the can but only four were released. The first of these came in August 1952, the second in March 1953. The first release featured the sorrowful Korean War opus "A soldier not in uniform" pitched with the upbeat "Will you welcome me there." By now Cheeks' voice had hardened but had not yet been worn to an anguished rasp. On "Will you welcome me there" Cheeks jousts with James but keeps reasonably fixed at the boundaries of being in control. "Will he welcome me there" drew attention due to an irresistible tempo but "A soldier not in uniform" became the most played side, partly due to its topical content. The country was also gearing up for its first hydrogen bomb test.

The second release of "I thank you Lord" backed by "A sinner's plea" brings us a different scenario. On "I thank you Lord" James wails and hollers against Jefferson's pumping bass plus a wall of high harmonies. Woodruff leads on "A sinner's plea" in Jeter-like style.

The 'Gales were put on an East Coast tour with the Bells of Joy. Both were booked through Don Robey's Buffalo Booking Agency run by the astute Evelyn Johnson. Robey's Duke Records' partner (up until late 1952) was David James Mattis. Mattis was a deejay on Memphis-based WDIA, the largest black-oriented radio station in the South. Through Mattis and others Robey was able to effectively spread the word, namely Peacock Gospel Records, throughout the Southern states. The Southern market was extremely important to Robey as sales in the Southlands constituted a significant overall percentage.

The Bells of Joy headlined on the East Coast tour because of the healthy sales of "Let's talk about Jesus" which eventually became one of Robey's first gospel best sellers. However, the 'Gales were still building kindling and by their second Houston session of October 1953 were ready to take on all major competition.

Cheeks was unhappy with the fact that the group was earning so little money. The Soul Stirrers were making overtures to enlist Cheeks' service. Cheeks' presence in the Soul Stirrers would have made the group unbeatable in every respect, both as a sweet-singing quartet captained by Sam Cooke and a church-wrecking crew led by 'June'

Cheeks.

Jo Jo Wallace says both Cheeks and Sam became close buddies. It was Sam who wanted Cheeks in the Soul Stirrers. Cheeks grabbed the chance of making a better living and jumped into the Soul Stirrers leaving Ernest James as solo lead vocalist. But the mixture of the rough and the smooth, coupled with the fact that Cheeks would prove unmanageable at times, did not work for the Soul Stirrers. Cheeks cut only one session with the Soul Stirrers on March 2nd, 1954. Sam and Cheeks shared leads on "All right now," a mid tempo burner in two parts. Cheeks' driving, emotional reading took Sam out of crooning and into heavier metal.

The release of the Sensational Nightingales' loping "God's word will never pass away" in November 1953 on Peacock (with Cheeks now returned to the group) set the stage for what was to come. Robey kept the boys busy by sending them out on a string of one-nighters through Arkansas, Louisiana, Kentucky and Indiana. The reverse of "God's word will never pass away" gave us "Does Jesus care," a song written by Kenneth Morris and lead by Cheeks with soul and compassion. Here we can feel the overwhelming strength of the man's matchless emotional reserve. What we should have experienced with "Does Jesus care" is a stretch into two parts.

By the close of this single-sider one wishes that a reverse second part would snatch up the song and take it (and us) to paradise. But Cheeks was held back and somehow never given a chance to work it with his magic. One can imagine how he would have worked the song if it had been done live in a church where most of the saints would inevitably have been sprawled out across their seats by the close of the performance.

We have to wait until May 1954 before going out and grabbing the next 'Gales release. Meanwhile, Robey's healthy spiritual sales, especially in the Southlands, helped increase visibility, not only for the 'Gales but others like the Bells of Joy from Austin, Christland Singers from Chicago, Dixie Hummingbirds from Philadelphia, Jessie Mae Renfro from Dallas and the Sunset Travelers from Memphis whom he kept on the road for as long as he could.

The May 1954 release of "I'm going on with Jesus" was awarded a four-star rating in Billboard's Spiritual Releases column, an honor few achieve. The reverse, "Another year," was given a three-star boost. "I'm going on with Jesus" is a wild, galloping opus, made of intricate rhythm patterns. Cheeks and James build up an emotional insanity until the tune reaches explosive limits.

"Another year" found Cheeks preaching in stop-time and singing in the mid-tempo range. His signature hard-throated scream took precedence over all else.

The Gales' following release was recorded in February 1954 but not issued until January 1955 when it was listed in Billboard's New Spiritual Releases column and awarded three stars top and bottom. This tepid rating was due in part to Robey's insistence on the group holding to arrangements that had proven fruitful in the past and not having the outfit try fresher and brighter ideas. Both Jo Jo Wallace and June Cheeks were gifted with excellent writing and arranging skills, but these were obviously set aside.

The record in question was "I'm serving the Lord" undersided with "Go where Jesus is." "I'm serving the Lord," a mid-tempo chart lead by James builds toward emotional catharsis. "Go where Jesus is" is a shared Cheeks-James vehicle, sung in the style of the reverse. One wishes that Cheeks had grabbed the last chorus and cut his chops on it.

It seems to me that Cheeks had been bridled or punished in some way because of his brief absence from the group.

Despite the fact that the 'Gales were doing well they always seemed to end up with little money in their pockets. Jo Jo Wallace relates that "We often had to put our nickels and dimes together so that we could fetch a loaf of bread a large bottle of soda and some baloney to make one sandwich and pass it around. We did this so often we gave it a name: 'quartet chicken' or sometimes 'bucket chicken.'"

In May 1955 Peacock issued "On the judgement day" backed with "Who will be the one." Both songs were from their pre-Cheeks defection's third session of February, 1954. "On the judgement day" is another Cheeks-James sparring, this time an echo-chamber effect had been added. Both Cheeks and James tried to out-sing each other on this mid-tempo burner that finds Cheeks at the peak of his saved and sanctified powers.

The flip of "On the judgement day," "Who will be the one," starts mournfully and builds as Cheeks adds more and more fire and brimstone. Stories were told of how Cheeks, soaked in sweat at the end of his performance, was carried off between two supporting soldiers to recover from death-defying physical exhaustion. It was never in June Cheeks' nature to offer less than all he could give and to support this super-human effort he turned to alcohol to ease the pain. He would rather give his last performance lying in a drunken stupor on his death-bed than do what the doctor told him to do. If ever a gospel singer gave much, few gave more. It was Wilson Pickett's mistake to follow in his footsteps.

As Cheeks reached the zenith of his vocal powers, his leads would follow the same unforgiving formula: anguished pleas and sanctified 'doomed-if-you-don't' lyrics, set against a pumping bass and a wall of hell's-own wailing voices in high register. This image of Cheeks reminds one of the Greek god, Prometheus, a titan chained and tortured by Zeus for stealing fire from heaven and giving it to man. Surrounded by squealing harpies, Cheeks struggled to enter paradise.

Jo Jo Wallace tells that "back in those days it was really rough. There weren't so many so-called professional groups traveling from state to state. There were only groups like the Pilgrim Travelers from Los Angeles, the Soul Stirrers out of Chicago, the two bunches of Blind Boys out of Alabama and Mississippi, the Dixie Hummingbirds out of Greenville and later Philadelphia and of course us, the Sensational Nightingales." Some of the lesser known groups were self-taught and gamely wanted to out-sing one another, hoping to get a break and sign a contract with a record company who would record their material. Thereby, they hoped to quickly make themselves popular enough to travel.

There was not much money being made but you could do much more with five dollars than you could do with fifty today. "So far as the Sensational Nightingales traveled, the spirit would touch people's hearts, because lots of times we stayed in their homes," says Jo Jo. "Many people felt like we were sent from heaven to bless them through our songs thinking we were singing prophets sent down to encourage and bless them spiritually. Some of them not only took us into their homes, they fed us good down-home country meals and sometimes gave us a place to sleep. We never did earn enough money to check in at hotels. First off, there were no hotels at the time for us colored folk to check into, even if we had money in our pockets to pay for the rooms. It was so rough that for many years we would often sleep in our old, second-hand cars which we got for two hundred dollars a pop. A few years later colored folks began running their own hotels, hotels they had made out of rooming houses they had rented from white folk."

Jo Jo Wallace goes on to say, "We had to ride on 'recap' tires, that was all we could afford. We drove many, many miles on these 'recap' tires which we called 'pop' or 'may pop' tires that could burst at any time. I remember we were driving on 'may pops.' I was sitting on the right side of the back seat. As we drove around a corner, I saw the right back tire pass me close by my window. I cried out 'Hey! Our tire just passed by my window!' The car fell on its side and rested on its rear axle. We replaced the tire with a 'may pop' we had in the trunk. We drove on through a town called LaGrange on West Point Lake, Georgia. We were speeding around the curves and noticed a Highway Patrol car through our rear window. It was flashing its lights for us to pull over. We pulled over to the side knowing full well we were speeding, but to our surprise the patrolman didn't mention the fact we were driving too fast. 'Take a look at your left back tire,' the patrolman said. We got out and saw that the inner tube had burst out of the rim of the wheel. It was an act of faith. Driving on a blow-out would have been fatal. We would have rolled over and over down the slope. We thanked the officer for saving us in time. Luckily we had another 'may pop' in the trunk. It was real cold that evening so we burned the old tire and the inner tube by the side of the road to keep us all warm."

"As time went by," continues Jo Jo, "June Cheeks and I became pretty close. We were a great team. I don't know how I came to get one but I managed to pick up a fifty foot extension chord to run from my guitar to the amp. Our mike set-up was such that three singers stood around a

mike at center stage while June and I stood off to the left
and right sides. During our act as the trio kept tight harmony June Cheeks would creep down the left aisle screaming and preaching and carrying on while I danced (I had
all Chuck Berry's moves down before he ever used them)
down the right aisle playing my guitar. Church-folk called
me 'The Gospel Chuck Berry' and as chance would have it,
I even looked a lot like him, especially when I had my hair
teased up in a pompadour. We created a lot of excitement
with this act.

Jo Jo states that the reason Ernest James was taken
on was to set up the crowd for June Cheeks. It sure looked
that way at times.

The Sensational Nightingales toured widely in the
Fifties. They traveled with Madam Edna Gallmon Cooke
filling in for her background group, the Southern Sons.
Jo Jo Wallace always remembers with a smile the time he
fell on a slippery stage when touring somewhere in Florida with Mdm Edna Gallmon Cooke. When Jo Jo hit the
ground Cooke burst out laughing so much she peed herself.
The event ended out with everyone falling about in peals of
laughter. Cooke later married their manager, Barney Parks.
Cooke's pianist, Marjorie (or Marge) married June Cheeks.
Marie Knight's sister, Bernice, married original Nightingales basso Bill Henry, and basso Carl Coates (who joined
the Nightingales in the late 1950s) married the great Dorothy Love of the Gospel Harmonettes. It seems that gospel
singers needed to pool their spiritual qualities in times
when such kinship was essential.

In June 1955 the 'Gales cut their landmark recording of "A Christian life" backed with the winning "Somewhere to lay my head." "A Christian life" garnered yet another four-star Billboard rating, while the equally exquisite

"Somewhere to lay my head" received a lesser three stars. For this writer, "A Christian life" is one of the Sensational Nightingales' all-time finest triumphs. Set against super-powered, high voltage, sweet-wailing, sky-lifting, howling voices and relentless pumping bass, Ernest James raises this song through the church roof up within earshot of the suspected Man Upstairs. "Somewhere to lay my head," fielded by June Cheeks, was the antithesis of the Highway Q.C.'s softer reading of May 1955. On the 'Gales' version, Cheeks grunts, growls and grabs you by the gut as if by the last stanza you still needed his anointing to get you there.

On December 15, 1955 the 'Gales were reported as having the distinction of appearing on Thurman Ruth's First Gospel Caravan at Harlem's Apollo Theatre alongside the Five Blind Boys of Mississippi, the Pilgrim Travelers, the Harmonizing Four, Brother Joe May and Christine Clark. Thurman Ruth had come up with the idea of regular gospel caravan shows during his appearance on a program with the Selah Jubilee Singers at the Apollo that same month. Ruth approached Apollo patriarch, Frank Schiffman, with an idea of gospel package shows presented in the same way as Murray Kaufman of WMCA presented rhythm and blues. Some gospel singers went with the idea, but others thought that taking gospel into a 'house of sin' was inappropriate. But then Ruth replied by quoting a passage from the Bible which read: "Go into the hedges and highways to compel men to come and be saved." You cannot argue with that.

The 'Gales appeared again on Ruth's caravan venued at the Lawson Auditorium. Frank Schiffman had double-booked with a second gospel package show put together by WWRL gospel disc jockeys Doc Wheeler and Fred Barr. WWRL won out over Ruth. Also appearing on the Lawson

Auditorium Ruth Caravan were the Five Blind Boys of Mississippi and the Swan Silvertones. The competition that day was fierce.

The Sensational Nightingales' next release surfaced in May 1956. This confection was made up of "Lord have mercy," a left-over from the October 1953 session, and "See how they done my Lord," recorded in March 1956. "Lord have mercy," a co-lead mid-tempo composition was concocted as were others to replicate the same winning formula as before. "See how they done my Lord" is a joyous-sounding Cheeks nugget centered on the Fascist passions of the Crucifixion, a less than joyous subject. However, Cheeks gave the song his full weight of worry.

At this point we have come to the 'Gales' second all-time spirit-killing masterpiece, "Burying ground" which Cheeks wielded in live performance to annihilate all competing quartets and convince everyone present that nobody, even Thor the God of Thunder, could beat out the 'Gales. Cheeks, one of the earliest exponents of long-chord crowd-creeping and confronting ladies up close with a stern and fully convicted countenance coupled with growling remonstrations, cut through his audience like a corn-cutting harvester. It was easy to imagine how overworked the uniformed church attendants must have felt as they dragged away the bodies of those who had fallen in a swoon or as Reverend Settle used to say, "had gone beyond the pop-off point."

"Burying ground" was released around Christmas 1956. It was the peak of prosperity for most citizens of the U.S. but eight months before the Congress passed the first Civil Rights Act. The underside of "Burying ground" gave us "In my mind," yet another demon slayer. First, with "Burying ground" one cannot fail to feel a spasm-like tingle

shoot up the spine or a shudder as the result of an inde-
scribable force overwhelming the listener's state of mind.
All this describes the way I feel when hearing "Burying
ground," one of the finest moments in recorded quartet history. The song, of course, is captained by June Cheeks and
sung so hard one is convinced that Cheeks had died and
risen from the dead, an apparition believed in by some In-
dian tribes people, perhaps Cheeks' own spiritual ancestors.
Many of Cheeks' immediate ancestors were indeed Native
Americans. Cheeks might have been able to recall a sacred
burying ground, known only to people in his tribe. "In my
mind" is another mid-tempo wailer emblazoned with the
usual but less intentional histrionics.

Now we turn to Jo Jo Wallace and his part in composing "The Twist." Back in Williamston during the Thirties Jo Jo listened to his sister "Minnie" Margaret singing a
tune called "Messin' around," a song made popular by Trix-
ie Smith on Paramount in 1926. "Minnie" Margaret would
use the 'twist' word in the song. In 1957 Jo Jo recalled the
incident and started playing around with it on guitar with
Bill Woodruff who helped out on making up fresh lyrics. Jo
Jo had penned the first line of the song, "C'mon baby, let's
do the twist." Being as Jo Jo was the member of a spiritual
group and did not want to use the song or cross over with
the Sensational Nightingales to R&B, he held on to the
tune. Jo Jo did, however, make one attempt to sell his fin-
ished song. This was to Little Joe Cook, but Cook was not
interested in recording it.

Somehow, David Edrington, who had just joined or
was in the process of joining the Sensational Nightingales
as tenor singer got hold of the song and brought it to the attention of Syd Nathan at King Records who, in turn, passed
it along to Hank Ballard and the Midnighters. Ballard,

together with his guitarist and arranger Cal Green, used the opening twist line as a jump off point to writing their own arrangement of "The Twist" which was a little different from Jo Jo's. The original Hank Ballard / Cal Green arrangement was recorded with the Midnighters at King Records in 1958. "The Twist" was re-recorded in January 1959 as a B-side to the vocal group ballad "Teardrops on your letter." After the song took off and became an enormous hit Jo Jo Wallace was asked if he had signed any song-writing agreement with King. He answered by saying he just let it go, adding that gospel music was his life and that rhythm and blues did not concern him. And so ends that saga.

January 1957 saw the release of yet another remarkable 'Gales recording, the awe-inspiring "I gave my heart to Jesus" with Cheeks' frightening, savage voice, as urgent and exciting as ever before. One cannot imagine finding any church lady standing after a live performance of this. So devastating were Cheeks' vocal incendiaries one can imagine unseen flames shooting out of his mouth.

The late Kip Anderson told me that when he went out as Clara Ward's touring pianist he often encountered Cheeks doing his work. He said that at one time when Cheeks was holding forth on a double show program (one show in the afternoon, another in the evening) that towards the close of the first show he would step off stage acting the clown, creeping and screaming into the audience, cutting his way like the grim reaper with a long-handled scythe. When he reached the door of the church he continued to creep on past the line waiting for the second show. Not only did he sing down the saints at the first show, he did the same with the line waiting for the second.

Both sides of the aforementioned single were awarded a four-star credential in Billboard but somehow did not sell that well. The flip-side, "I'm coming up Lord" was a righteous chart driven by a pumping bass.

Jo Jo Wallace was always complaining about Cheeks' driving skills, or lack thereof. On one occasion, when Jo Jo sat next to him in the front seat, Cheeks fell asleep while driving at a rapid speed and narrowly avoided colliding into the rear end of an eighteen-wheeler truck. As a joke, he remarked "I was just taking me a fifteen minute nap!" And laughed it off. Cheeks was losing his marbles.

Besides this he was really tired of the racist problems encountered when touring through the Southlands. On one occasion the 'Gales' car was stopped on a highway near Corinth, Mississippi by the Highway Patrol. Jo Jo referred to them as 'our white brothers,' a gross mis-statement. Two officers got out of their car and taunted them with expletives and racial slurs. Jo Jo remarked that he kept his cool because they were just waiting for them to make the wrong move. The officers were further inflamed when, after pulling out two persons from the back seat with what they thought were scarves but were in fact doo-rags tied around their heads, they found that the two passengers were male and black and not white women. One officer had his weapon drawn and was asking what they were doing there. Jo Jo timidly replied, "We're all singing the gospel." "We don't need it down here – we've got these niggers under control," replied the patrolman. Jo Jo could not help but burst out into loud peals of laughter. The officer seemed not to mind that Jo Jo thought they were making a joke and let the party go. But the 'Gales never wanted to go back to Mississippi after that.

At this point the group was touring with the Swan Silvertones. Jo Jo and Bill Woodruff were sitting in the back of the car, Dewey Young and June Cheeks sat up front. Jo Jo recalls that Dewey Young sometimes sang with the 'Gales during this period when extra souls were needed, but he never recorded with them. The same can be said about Tommy Ellison who is even seen in promotional photographs with the Sensational Nightingales but as far as I know never recorded with the group.

During the time that Tommy Ellison was singing with the Sensational Nightingales Jo Jo remembers stopping for gas only to be met by an attendant armed with a shotgun. "No gas here!" he shouted.

The 'Gales only had to wait twelve weeks before the release of their next single which was "Pressing on." The only personnel change after June Cheeks' return was that Ernest James quit. I do not think June Cheeks was too happy having his style crimped. "Pressing on" was twinned with "View that holy city." "Pressing on" is a jumpy number rendered ruggedly by the man with the steel voice. "View that holy city" begins with an unidentified tenor lead – could this be Tommy Ellison's only appearance on vinyl as lead with the group? Cheeks picks up the song midway but never gets time to set it ablaze.

Right on the heels of "Pressing on" Robey elected to rush out "The Lord will make a way" coupled with "To the end." The echo-enhanced "The Lord will make a way" is a mid-tempo hymn sung overall pretty much in standard style. On the other hand, "To the end" rocks the soul of the church with Cheeks' cheerful, raspy stanzas and his wife's stomping piano that never fails to drive the tune along like a well-stoked engine. A live rendering of the song filmed in 1964 for TV Gospel Time shows Cheeks and the Four Knights supported by his wife playing this song with her elbows. One catches her dazzling black gown lined with sparkling silver crosses, a sight one finds hard to forget.

February 1958 marked the expansion of Don Robey's Duke and Peacock recording empire. A strong sales, promotion and distribution network was set up on the East Coast and plans were being laid for the manufacture of Duke and Peacock blues and gospel albums.

The Sensational Nightingales cut two more singles before the release of their first album. The first of these was June Cheeks' beseeching "Can I count on you" sandwiched with the overwhelming "A closer walk with Thee" which includes the most soulfully penetrating sermonette Cheeks ever recorded. The second issue was Cheeks holding forth on "Who is that" and "Over in Zion." Cheeks' voice was showing signs of serious damage at this juncture. Carl Coates was now replaced by John Jefferson on the bass part.

The line-up for the "Songs of Praise" album (Peacock 101, 1960) included Jo Jo Wallace, tenor and guitar, Bill Woodruff, baritone, David Edrington, tenor, June Cheeks, lead baritone and Carl Coates or John Jefferson, bass.

This essential collectors' album found subsequent release in England, France and Germany and is up there in the best twenty Post-War gospel quartet albums as one of the top five. Nine new cuts were recorded for the album itself. The remaining "Burying ground" and "To the end" were from singles cut in 1956 and 1957. It is amazing that a top tier quartet should cut so few recordings over the course of seven years. We realize that the group toured constantly, but the fact that they enjoyed only nine known recording sessions during all this time is a little puzzling. Despite management problems with Cheeks who really did not get along with manager Barney Parks Cheeks wore himself ragged and eventually required hospitalization.

The group could have been taped at any number of studios or in concert. June Cheeks was a musical legend and was also renowned for his womanizing. But on stage he gave too much to stay on top. He tried making a comeback in 1966 but he could not cut it and had to be let loose. Cheeks' last Gales-related recording in 1959 was the song "Rock of Ages" supported by Jo Jo Wallace on guitar and an unheralded vocal group. The song first showed up on a Songbird Peacock subsidiary various artists album some eleven years later. The album was called "Mother's Favorite Songs" (Songbird 230) and is well worth trying to find.

Two Sensational Nightingales songs from the "Songs of Praise" album, "I want to know" and the exquisite "What would you give," wound up on a Peacock single.

When Cheeks left the 'Gales in 1960 the outfit encountered all kinds of problems. Who do we get to fill June Cheeks' shoes? They tried out a number of would-be contenders including Big Henry Johnson who wound up with the Blind Boys of Mississippi in 1963, Willie Banks who was around for a few live gigs, and Otis Clay who made it as far as auditioning for the Sensational Nightingales' second album, Peacock PLP 112, entitled "Glory Glory." The final choice came down to a different style of vocalist altogether, Charles Johnson. Johnson was Cheeks' choice. Cheeks much admired his song-writing and country-like approach to singing.

According to Jo Jo Wallace, June Cheeks spent a short while with the Blind Boys of Alabama before forming and joining the Four (Gospel) Knights, but it would be two years before Johnson finally made it onto the Gales team. When June Cheeks formed the Four Gospel Knights in 1962 they were billed on his initial Peacock recording as "and singers." This original group was mighty indeed as they were made up of some of the finest and strongest gospel singers of the time – tenor Arthur Lee "Bob" Beatty (who had come from the Trumpets of Joy along with master basso Providence Thomas), Horace Thompson (who later joined the 'Gales) and the great Dewey Young (who had just disbanded the fabulous Flying Clouds, a.k.a. Divine Travelers.

This dynamite bunch headed up by Cheeks gave us two stunning singles releases on Peacock in 1962. These were "What a morning" and "A mother's plea" plus "Holy wine" coupled with "Tomorrow's sun." The four songs appeared on a French Vogue extended play release. This was Cheeks at his unrestrained best and constitutes two of the finest gospel quartet releases of that year.

In 1963, with the group now confirmed as the Four Gospel Knights with Cheeks' wife added on piano, Peacock issued two more fully anguished singles. Songs include the much celebrated "Last mile of the way" and "Mother sang these songs." Both became staples on Cheeks' later live appearances.

1964-1965 brought us "Waiting (for my child to come home)" and "Somewhere around God's throne." By now the strain on Cheeks' vocal chords was beginning to sound painful. But Cheeks soldiered on, with two further sessions from 1967-1968 and 1969. My personal favorites include "How far is heaven" and "Get my child out of jail" from the 1967-1968 session and "Where do I go from here" and "Like a tramp on the street" from 1969. Thirteen of the fourteen songs issued from these two last Peacock sessions appeared on the two albums listed in the annotated albums section of this book.

It is a sin that MCA, who currently owns the rights to this material, does not issue a complete Julius Cheeks and the Four Gospel Knights CD collection. We have to be content with the reissue of Rev. Julius Cheeks Sings ...

(Peacock LP 164) on MCA MF2-760, "Raisin the Roof," mixed (3 artists) collection issued back in 1992.

Cheeks broke up the original Four Gospel Knights in 1970 and for five years went into semi-retirement, spending most of his time as residing minister at his church in Baltimore, Maryland. Ignoring doctors' warnings, he tried to make a come-back in 1975 with the release of a Su-Ann album, One Of These Days We'll All Be Home (see the annotated gospel album discography.) Cheeks died in Miami on January 21st, 1981.

The 1960/1961 post-Cheeks 'Gales lineup included Jo Jo Wallace, tenor and guitar, Herbert Robinson, tenor (who also served as Cheeks' temporary replacement), David Edrington, second tenor lead, Bill Woodruff, baritone and Carl Coates, bass. This configuration of the 'Gales cut two singles over an eighteen month period. The first was Robinson's "Canaan land" sung in sanctified spirit against Coates' excellent pumping bass and strong support from the rhythm section. The B-side, "In the presence of the Lord," follows the same shout formula with David Edrington working up the song.

The second single was released after the reissue of the two aforementioned Cheeks sides from "Songs of Praise." Here we have Edrington's workout on the hymn-like "People I used to see" partnered with Robinson's soulful passion on "The storm is passing over." The coupling of Edrington and Robinson after Cheeks' departure seemed like working out pretty well but once a new path was chosen and Charles Johnson was taken into the fold in 1962 the lineup evolved into Jo Jo Wallace, tenor and guitar, Charles Johnson replacing Edrington, baritone, Herbert Robinson, first tenor lead, Bill Woodruff, baritone and Carl Coates, bass. David Edrington passed away in 1962, soon after his departure from the group.

Discussion of the subsequent albums recorded by the Sensational Nightingales can be found for the most part in the Discography. Only the singles, many of which ended up on long play anyway, have been discussed here.

Charles Johnson and the Sensational Nightingales / Revivers

Charles Johnson Jnr. was born the last of five children to Mamie and Charles Johnson in 1931, on the fairly expansive Donel Ranch near Paris, Texas in Lamar County. Mamie and Charles Snr. were sharecroppers. Times were hard, and the country was suffering the worst days of the Depression. Seeking a better life, Charles Snr. took up and left shortly after Junior was born, leaving Mamie, who already worked in the ranch owners' house, to raise the five kids and take charge of the ranch and farm. The family grew corn, sugarcane and cotton with little more than mules to turn the soil in the fields. Young Charles Jnr. took a special interest in the horses. From the time he could walk he was out in the stables tending to the animals or riding across the plains on the back of his favorite charge. Charles ran errands and did his share of farm work.

The boy's early musical impressions were picked up on a small, cheap battery radio. His strongest recollections were of listening to the Grand Ole Opry and country music programming out of Nashville. (This would account for the fact that his music always reflected his love of country hymns.) But he also caught the weekly Golden Gate Quartet broadcasts. Various uncles and cousins sang in local gospel quartets, principally the Harmony Kings of Paris, Texas (not to be confused with the famous quartet from Orangeburg, South Carolina.) One can envision the young Charles riding bare-back and singing country songs across the Texas plains, but this was not always the case. He also attended the family church which was the A.M.E. Methodist and sang in the choir.

At the age of sixteen Charles Junior went to work as a regular ranch hand riding and mending fences on the 100-acre Merc Davis Ranch of West Texas between Albany and Abilene in Shackelford County. Charles took to the work like a duck to water and was soon given the job of breaking in horses, a task he loved with a passion.

A year later, moving ten miles northwest, he went to work on the Green family ranch where he was taken in and treated like an adopted son. It was here that Charles found his calling and a desire to sing church music as a profession. He occasionally sang in local gospel groups.

In 1950 the Greens died in an automobile accident while on vacation. Charles was devastated and could not bear the thought of working the ranch with the Greens gone. Moving to Lubbock, Texas in 1950 Charles played semi-pro football and kept up his interest in singing by joining a local quartet managed by businessman Robert H. Hood. Hood also sang in the group. Calling themselves the Loving Five, the outfit was composed of bass singer Marshall Cooper and brother Richmond, Early Williams, Augusta Chisholm and Charles. The Cooper father played on the L.A. Lakers basketball team. Hood moved to Pasadena, California and wanted the group to follow him out. Not all Loving Five members could as easily pull up stakes and move away from home. Only Charles Johnson and Marshall Cooper made the trip west, thus breaking up the original Loving Five.

In Pasadena, Hood reformed the quartet and switched their name to the Gospel Consolators, adding Haskell Holmes and Reo Watson. The Gospel Consolators at first played local venues but traveled farther afield as their reputation grew by leaps and bounds. Various singers moved in and out of the group, including Jesse Hill who was thought to have recorded with a second group calling themselves the Gospel Consolators. This group, probably made up of local San Francisco Bay Area singers, cut three records for Bob Geddins' Big Town label out of East Oakland in late 1955. However, upon listening to these sides, one is struck with an older approach to singing more akin to Post-War jubilee, unlike any of the recordings Johnson's group made around this period.

In 1955, Robert H. Hood and Reo Watson formed a record company, H. & W. Records, to promote the repertoire of the Gospel Consolators. It was easier for a gospel quartet, especially a semi-professional one like the Gospel Consolators, to find work if etchings of their songs were out there for the benefit of the record-buying public. The group usually sang on weekends. Johnson drove a delivery truck during the week. He even tried his hand at boxing and competed for the Golden Gloves title but soon realized that singing was a surer way of staying alive in one piece.

Johnson and the Gospel Consolators cut three records for H. & W. during the course of one year. The makeup of the group at this time was Joseph Dumas and Charles Johnson sharing lead vocals, Robert H. Hood, Reo Watson, Haskell Holmes, Spencer Jackson and Oscar Cook (Sam Cooke's cousin) who had sung in the Varieteers, Chosen Gospel Singers and the Swan Silvertones. Johnson sang lead on "Do you know Him," "Sending up my timber" and "One more river" with emotional depth and conviction. Johnson, who considered himself primarily a songwriter and message-giver, always put more weight behind getting his message across in a natural way than using theatrical devices as a means of dramatic reinforcement.

As the group's reputation grew they found themselves on venues with the Mighty Clouds of Joy who were just gaining local attention and later (a year after the group had turned professional) Reverend Julius Cheeks and the Sensational Nightingales. Cheeks was impressed with the Gospel Consolators. In early 1959 he introduced the Gospel Consolators to Don Robey at Peacock Records in Houston.

The Gospel Consolators enjoyed three sessions at the Peacock studios over a period of as many years. Results from the final session hit the streets some time after Johnson and the group split up and had gone their separate ways. Members at this final period included Johnson and basso Nathaniel Bills, lead vocals, Cook, Hood and Dumas. Johnson sang his best realized work with the Gospel Consolators during this period. "Hold on to God's hand," "Who should remember," "Who is He" and "He won't let you down" are all message songs of passion, creative insight and depth of soul.

The Gospel Consolators found themselves on tour quite frequently with the Sensational Nightingales. Cheeks during the course of many intimate conversations asked Johnson whether he would take his place in the 'Gales. Johnson made it clear that he was not a rough and hard singer like Cheeks and that the group would have to deal with fans in the same way Sam Cooke had to deal with Rebert Harris's followers back in 1950 when it was quite clear that Cooke would be steering the Soul Stirrers in quite a different direction. Johnson would in stages make a softer soundprint with the 'Gales and at the same time retain as much integrity as Cheeks had mustered.

In time, Jo Jo Wallace and the 'Gales learned to accept this and indeed found that the group's gradually evolving new sound was one that appealed just as much, if not more, than that which went before. Besides, the 'Gales never had to worry about Johnson's voice ever running ragged.

When the Gospel Consolators fell apart in 1961, both Robert H. Hood and Joseph Dumas wound up back in Arkansas. In Little Rock, Dumas married one of the Loving Sisters, a gospel group who also made its mark on Peacock Records. Oscar Cook retired, and Haskell Holmes joined the Sweet Singing Cavaliers. Holmes can be heard singing falsetto-like high tenor on the Cavaliers' Savoy and Sharp recordings.

Johnson was gradually eased into the 'Gales. Only one side of his debut single with them featured him in ensemble performance. This was the cheerful, mid-tempo "Right now for Jesus." Robey chose to place a reissue for the underside. This was June Cheeks' pewburner "Blood for me" first issued on a former lineup's first album titled "The blood for Jesus." "The blood for Jesus" is one of Cheeks' most formidable charts, a spine-tingling experience for those who heard it and a transformation for those who witnessed it rendered on the concert stage.

Not yet wanting to stray too far from the previously successful formula, Johnson closely followed every one of Cheeks' vocal inflections on the third single release which gave us the upbeat "All be over." Although less Cheeks-like, it is still a tough-to-tell on the throat-thrashing passages. The reverse, "Don't put off today," is in fact a sanctified version of Will L. Thompson's "Softly and tenderly" done up in the old 'Gales tradition. The spirit of the group's old Southern hymn style is being followed here to the last note.

We get almost a repeat formula with the next single release of "Behold God's face" coupled with the break-neck tempo, church-stomping "(Need) More power" helmed by Robinson, the perfect piece of music to dust the house or aid a healthy workout. Herbert Robinson died shortly after the release of the "Glory Glory" 'Gales album. By this point Johnson was well along with his songwriting abilities. Robinson was briefly replaced by second tenor Rudolph Leamon, Johnson, Jo Jo Wallace, Thompson, Woodruff and Coates were all still in place and Arthur Crume from the Crume Brothers Quartet was added as bass guitar. This was the last set of 'unsettled' soldiers before the group solidified around Thompson, Jo Jo Wallace, Johnson and Woodruff in 1965.

Three life-changing events took place for Jo Jo Wallace during 1964. These were the marriage to his sweetheart Inez, the fact that he found himself born again and his move to Durham, North Carolina with his wife. Inez Evelyn Jones Wallace, Jo Jo's wife, was born in Fayetteville, North Carolina, the second of eleven children. She married Jo Jo in August 1964. She preferred to stay in the background, never wanting to interfere with Jo Jo's ministry. She passed in August 2009.

1964 was the same year that the Gales recorded their "Travel On" album. Four songs were taken from it for two singles releases. The first gave us Johnson's heartaching rendition of "Travel on" coupled with his narrative-like opus centered around the Crucifixion called "Never said a word."

Johnson's second single on Peacock found the soul-stretching "His great love" penned by himself (a song of considerable beauty) coupled with the church-rocking "Cleanse my soul" on which Johnson sings about the blessed gathered around the spiritual master and makes a joyful treat of it. Moving into 1965 and 1966 the 'Gales give us two more singles. Three of the four songs appear on later albums. The first release satisfies us with Johnson's "New Jerusalem," a mid-tempo opus once again penned by Johnson which finds him in a soulful and bluesy mood. "Going on just the same" on the reverse sounds like another upbeat chart styled on the usual Cheeks model, in fact it is difficult to tell Cheeks and Johnson apart.

"I'm so happy," also a 1966 release, undersided with "Prayed too late" followed. "Prayed too late," a pretty ballad delivered in the usual hymn-like style, sold well for the 'Gales and wound up on the 1967 album release entitled "Prayed Too Late." "I'm so happy" is a jolly jumper celebrating one's acceptance of Jesus Christ. The 'Gales' first 1967 single gave us "His truth (is marching on)," a ballad whose lyrics are composed of passages from the Good Book. "Walls of Jerusalem," a Christian's march around Jerusalem's impregnable walls, is effectively conveyed and takes up the reverse side of "His truth."

Forward to 1968 and the release of "Saints hold on," a song concerning man's need to cling to his faith. This is twinned with "The golden streets," or those heavenly freeways paved permanently with golden asphalt. It is good that the Lord thought about saving souls before committing his saved brethren to horrendous car repair bills. The 'Gales' glorious cover of Mrs. M.P. Ferguson's "Blessed quietness" plus Johnson's own "One faith, one God, one baptism" came out at the close of 1969. "One faith, one God, one baptism" is an extremely bluesy ballad punctuated with Jo Jo Wallace's righteous guitar fills. The group moans along in eerie harmony, a departure from the 'Gales' usual bag.

One of my favorite ballad renderings is the 'Gales' own "A heart like Thine" on which Johnson sings softly and tenderly and with unquestionable conviction. This 1970 release is coupled with Johnson's unforgettable reading of the traditional "It's gonna rain." Johnson had by now reached the climax of his songwriting and arranging powers and had presented us with a jewel of a gospel song. It had taken him eight years with the 'Gales to finally reach this extraordinary apex.

On the second 1970 'Gales single release we find reissue of "It's gonna rain" (for it must have sold like hot biscuits during its first release) backed with "At the meeting," yet another storytime session centered around the Almighty One's throne. The album version has the song extended to four and a half minutes. Jo Jo Wallace stated at the time that disc jockeys liked "It's gonna rain" because it was a down-to-earth good message song. But then most of the group's songs were message songs. The simple fact is that nothing quite matched the soul-grabbing sweetness of "A heart like mine" and "It's gonna rain."

The "It's Gonna Rain" album released in 1972 took off almost immediately and the sales re-established the Sensational Nightingales as being one of the country's finest hymn-centered, traditional black gospel quartets. The "It's Gonna Rain" album was also issued in celebration of Peacock's twentieth anniversary. All of this success occurred despite the absence of cornerstone pumping basso singer Carl Coates who moved in and out of the group regularly. The 'Gales had pared themselves down to a quartet and it seemed that things worked better that way. We also begin to notice the group's shift into a simpler mode, inspired by more Bible references with humble, convincing interpretations from the Southern white songbook, notably the inclusion of songs like "Where could I go" and "The last mile" from the Stamps-Baxter repertoire.

The Sensational Nightingales not only traversed the length and breadth of the nation but ventured abroad appearing on festivals and in concert halls in France, German, Switzerland and throughout Europe where the boys often appeared on programs with African American pop and R&B acts. During this time Johnson met the love of his life, Annie. They married and adopted two children. Close on the coattails of the highly successful "It's Gonna Rain Again" album Robey put out a collection entitled "You and I and Everyone." Four entries of particular merit make the album worthy of joining anyone's gospel album collection. The songs were: the title track "You and I and everyone," a "Standing at the judgement"-like composition done up in a web of good, tightly knitted harmony, "Face to face," a personal testimony, "I once was a stranger" rendered in old-time country gospel fashion reminiscent of the work of the Blackwood Brothers or Statesmen Quartet and finally "Take your burdens to the Lord (and leave them there)," a coaxingly rendered ballad perfected in a tender and humble way.

On May 21st, 1973, a short while before the launch of the "You and I and Everyone" album, Don Robey of Peacock Records and his partner, the ABC Record Corporation of New York, drew up an agreement for the transfer of Robey's assets to the major conglomerate. Robey's desire to sell out stemmed in part from his wanting to retire (he was now seventy years old) plus the costly lawsuit involving the Five Blind Boys of Mississippi, the late Reverend Robert Ballinger and Chess Records who were accused of spiriting the two artists away while under contract with Peacock Records. Robey had been placed under contract with ABC which stipulated that he did not have the power to go beyond his assistance in an advisory capacity. Chess interpreted this as being simply an information person and not one who deals with the business of contracts. As it turned out, Robey did not have to wait too long to have his problems resolved. He succumbed to a fatal heart attack on Monday June the 16, 1975. Unfortunately most of the day-to-day

Duke and Peacock correspondence, contract agreements, photos and sessions details were junked, tossed out in large Dumpsters, making it almost impossible to conduct accurate future research.

However, the 'Gales continued to put out soulfully inspired albums. In 1974 Johnson, Thompson, Jo Jo Wallace and Woodruff came together for the making of a new album release called "I Know Not the Hour." The set contained the beautiful, Biblical masterpiece "Mother Mary and Joseph," the delightfully exuberant "Love lifted me" composed by James Rowe and Howard E. Smith plus Horace Thompson's deeply soulful reading of Charles A. Tindley's "Nothing between." One is amazed by the fact that the "I Know Not the Hour" album failed to raise more notice. Somehow the fickle record-buying public did not feel the want to rush out in droves to buy this truly sensational collection.

The 1974 release of the "My Sisters and Brothers" album told a different story. Johnson's prayerful way with the title cut sent gospel record collectors back to the record stores. Other album standouts, beside the title track, include Jo Jo Wallace's soulful testimonial "If you strayed away," Horace Thompson's heartaching remonstration on "He'll make a way," and Johnson's whispered, sugary vocals on the Negro National Anthem – "Lift every voice and sing" supported expertly with throat-grunting ensemble harmony and Jo Jo Wallace's delicately ringing guitar.

Almost all of the group's ABC-Peacock album recordings were produced by Ira Tucker of the Dixie Hummingbirds which may account for the fine body of work. The 'Gales had reached fresh peaks of perfection when the following "Almighty Hand" album collection came out in 1975. By now the quartet had mastered a closeness in harmony very few traditional quartets could muster. The group's deep-country synchronization on "It's my desire" make this Thomas A. Dorsey anthem their very own. "Standing on the promises" is lead with depth and warmth of feeling by Johnson while group supports like a band of angels. Thompson and Johnson heap on the sorrow while rudimentary accompaniment orchestrates a lilting arrangement of "He hideth my soul." A remake of the old June Cheeks chestnut "What would you give" (Peacock 1829, 1959) is given a peerless, plaintive treatment.

ABC stuck to the ABC-Peacock logo on their gospel album releases for three years after Robey's demise in 1975. However, the Sensational Nightingales only enjoyed two album releases during this time. The first was "See You in the Rapture" which conveyed more simply rendered country style hymns with a title track featuring Johnson and Thompson trading verses against Jo Jo Wallace's narrative and a broad-sounding harmonic foundation. "Blessed Calvary" followed the same formula without Thompson's intercession. Thompson bares his soul on "Thank God I've been sealed" and "Oh how I love Jesus," both set in waltz tempo.

Released in 1978 with longer and less track selection, the group's final ABC album, "Jesus is Coming," is as firmly rooted in straight-ahead four part singing and Bible study as previous output. Johnson wails and moans on "Saved by Grace," colored with Jo Jo Wallace's bluesy guitar accompaniment. "Hard fighting soldier" again finds the group in strident harmony, an excellent remake of the 1964 original. "Learning to lean," righteously led by Horace Thompson, takes us back to the traditional four-part configuration with the reminder that the group rarely sweetened its songs with sweeping overlays of strings and complex choral embellishments. "Bad storm a raging," with its soulful melody and countrified accompaniment, brings us the 'Gales at their best. Jo Jo Wallace sermonizes on "How to be born again, and a strong blues riff and just plain, fine singing augment "Another river to cross."

With the demise of Peacock Records not long after Robey's death, its impressive roster of major traditional gospel artists was scattered to the winds. The Dixie Hummingbirds ended up on Atlanta International Records, Reverend Cleophus Robinson went with Belmark, the Mighty Clouds of Joy with Intersound Entertainment, the Blind Boys of Mississippi with Soul-Potion and the Jackson Southernaires, Pilgrim Jubilees and Sensational Nightingales went over to Tommy Couch and Jerry Mannery at Savgos / Malaco Records on Northside Drive in Jackson, Mississippi.

The Malaco label was founded in 1968, but its promotion and booking agency was set up beforehand in 1965. The label's first recordings were made at the celebrated Fame Studios in Muscle Shoals, Alabama just east along Highway 72 from Tuscambia where Couch was born and raised. Their first big-selling productions were King Floyd's "Groove me" on Couch's own Chimneyville label in 1970 and "Mr. Big Stuff" by Jean Knight leased to Stax in 1971. Couch's first venture into gospel music came about with the signing of the Jackson Southernaires in 1975.

After the Sensational Nightingales' ABC-Peacock contract expired in 1979 they signed with Couch through Dave Clark. Clark had been Don Robey's national promotions manager and had founded Robey's gospel subsidiary in 1964. Clark had also worked as producer with stellar gospel talent on Peacock and Nashboro Records out of Nashville. Although Malaco deals in blues and R&B as well as gospel, Couch asserts that it is his work with traditional gospel artists that most satisfies his personal tastes.

The Sensational Nightingales presented themselves in concert as being extremely professional, genuinely motivated and well organized. Johnson sang first lead and rarely played guitar during this time. Jo Jo Wallace took care of the sermonizing, played simple chording on guitar, and kept the guys in key. Thompson took on second lead chores and accompanied on bass guitar. Woodruff stuck to singing harmonies. A drummer was employed on occasion to fatten and strengthen the rhythm section.

The group always dressed immaculately and sometimes wore cummerbunds. Their harmonies were always as close as a zipper, and dignified choreography captivated the audience at every concert. With Malaco's first album release, "All About Jesus," Haran Griffin and Brian Williams were brought in to broaden the harmonies at the request of Dave Clark and Frank Williams, the producers. The late Frank(lin) Williams shared lead in the Jackson Southernaires and honed his skills as producer on many Malaco projects. Two of the album's compositions, "Crossroads of confusion" and "Hallelujah to the King," were performed by the Sensational Nightingales in the White Line Pictograph Production of the movie "Music Box," not the Costa Gavras 1989 fiasco, but a celluloid parable centering around a factory worker, five gospel singing angels (played by the Sensational Nightingales) and a music box.

"Crossroads of confusion" is a pretty ballad song calling all sinners to come home to God. "Because He lives," "Remind me, dear Lord," and "Strayed away" (Part 2) take us down the same road of sin and redemption. The group's magic touches hearts and stirs souls. The 1981 "Saints Hold On" album, again produced by Frank Williams aided by

Rev. Haran Griffin's arrangements and keyboards, is another song-fest filled with heart songs and joyous ballads done up in country gospel fashion. Drummer Brian Williams was added into the mix. "The straight way is narrow," "Oh Lord, I am depending on you," "He just hung there," "My house is full" and a remake of the traditional "Savior, don't pass me by" are all rendered with soul and grace. As always, Jo Jo Wallace and Johnson share in the song writing and arranging.

"He Is Real" (1982) was Johnson's third and final Malaco collection with the Sensational Nightingales. By this point an unmistakable refinement had been reached. The pleasant addition of piano makes this album a joy to listen to. Jo Jo Wallace's and Johnson's songs, as usual, are both delicate and soulfully inspired. Standouts include "His hand in mine," "Sweet forever land," "Do you know the man," "When we walk with the Lord," and Rev. E.S. Ufford's "Throw out the life line."

In late 1983, Johnson broke away from the Sensational Nightingales and was replaced by Calvert NcNair Jr., a similar-sounding vocal stylist. "Johnson is a unique writer and arranger who believes in the word of the Bible," says Jo Jo Wallace. "He left the Sensational Nightingales to spread the ministry in different areas," he added. With no bus, bookings or equipment, Johnson formed the Revivers in January 1984. With the tail end of a Malaco contract to go, the Revivers with the Luster Brothers, Darrell and Rick, recorded their first and only Malaco album entitled "No Man Can Stand Up Alone" (1984.) Johnson's idea of building a group around himself was to support his wish to stick to his Southern gospel roots.

The trio's third release, "One night revival," on Better-Way Records out of Hollister, North Carolina was recorded and video taped live at The Dayton Memorial Hall in Dayton, Ohio. The threesome playing to a mixed, packed house moved the people with genuine heartfelt soul and good old down-home black country gospel music. Johnson states that the reason Dayton was picked for their first live concert video recording was that they had made legions of fans in that part of the Buckeye state.

By 1986, the first set of Revivers was gone and replaced by three young fellows by the names of Gary Miles, Melvin Wilson and Greg Logins. Material was now being produced by Johnson and Terry Exley. The Revivers' style had entered the mainstream with the addition of two electronic keyboard players and a slew of updated arrangements that appealed more to a younger listener.

By 1995, Miles, Wilson, and Logins were gone and replaced by Michael Watts and Tracy Pierce from Florida. On the Canaan release of "I believe," Theresa Burton, Kay Ferguson, and Jack Russell were added to fill out vocal backgrounds. "I believe" with its heavy percussive overlays and female choral embellishments is more a showcase for Charles Johnson's solo endeavors than to front a set of three or four voices in harmony. In fact, choral treatments have now replaced any recognizable harmonic quartet support.

By this point the Sensational Nightingales over at Malaco had reached the 'gospel icons' status. Not only did they perform at the Smithsonian Institute in Washington, D.C., they participated in a panel discussion regarding the history of black gospel singers and gospel singing black history.

The North Carolina-based Revivers group was stabled with the Harper and Associates Booking Agency in Goodletville, Tennessee. Their tour bus usually took off on three-day engagements Thursdays through Saturdays or Fridays through Sundays depending on schedule. The group played both church and concert hall venues on a year round basis, leaving little time to relax with their respective families. Members in 1996, aside from Johnson (lead vocals and rhythm guitar), were Joe Yancey from New England who doubled on drums, Steve Boyd from Missouri who split talents between singing harmonies and playing keyboards, Maurice Morgan Snr. from North Carolina who likewise sung and played lead guitar, and Tracy Pierce who divided between harmonies and bass guitar.

Annotated Album Discography: Nightingales / Sensational Nightingales (1959-1982) / Rev. Julius Cheeks plus Charles Johnson and the Revivers

King LP 576 – "Spirituals, Vol. 5" (1958)
– Trumpeteers, Nightingales, Patterson Singers

Ben Joyner (tenor), Paul Owens (tenor lead / manager), Howard Carroll (baritone / guitar) and William Henry (bass)

* 5 selections, sung traditionally in the Jubilee style lead by Paul Owens from December 1949

Spirit Feel 1001 – "Father and Sons"
– Five Blind Boys of Mississippi / Sensational Nightingales / Soul Stirrers

Ben Joyner (tenor), Paul Owens (tenor lead / manager), Howard Carroll (baritone / guitar), William Henry (bass) and Julius Cheeks (baritone & second lead)

* 1 selection, "There's a vacant room in Heaven" lead by Julius Cheeks from 1951 (plus three later cuts from Peacock 1955-1956 rendered by a slightly different lineup)

Peacock 101 – "Songs of Praise" (1960)
– Sensational Nightingales

* With varying personnel; the cream of the sanctified Julius Cheeks experience from sessions cut in 1956 with "Burying ground," (1957) with "To the end," plus the monumental 1959/1960 session which gave us "Standing at the judgement," "What would you give," "The blood of Jesus," and others. The pinnacle of the group's spiritual power. Absolutely essential collectors' item

Peacock 112 – "Glory, Glory" (1963) – Sensational Nightingales

Horace Thompson (tenor), Joseph "Jo Jo" Wallace (tenor / guitar), Charles Johnson (lead tenor), Herbert Robinson (or Robertson) (baritone), Bill Woodruff (baritone) and Carl Coates (bass).

* Charles Johnson's softer, soul-warming debut album containing such standouts as "Behold God's face," "Wonderful time up there" and "End of my journey" penned by Johnson and Robertson

Peacock 118 – "Travel On" (1964) – Sensational Nightingales

Rudolph Leamon and Horace Thompson (tenors), Joseph "Jo Jo" Wallace (tenor / guitar), Charles Johnson (tenor / baritone lead), Arthur Crume (baritone / second guitar & bass guitar), Bill Woodruff (baritone), Carl Coates (bass)

* More Johnson gems with Johnson writing and Jo Jo arranging with nuggets like "When Jesus comes," "Travel on" and "His great love"

Peacock 131 – "Prayed Too Late" (1965-1967) – Sensational Nightingales

Thompson, Wallace, Johnson and Woodruff with and without Carl Coates (bass)

* A rough, mid-Sixties period with the core of the music encountering drastic changes. Despite this, great soul-warming gems prevail like "He prayed too late," Son of God" and "The love of Jesus"

Peacock 137 – "The Best Of" (1967) – Sensational Nightingales

* A selection of the best in reissue format stretching from 1956 to 1967. A fabulous retrospective

Peacock 140 – "Golden Gems of Gospel: the World's Greatest Spiritual and Gospel Artists" (1967)

* With retreads of "Morning train" and "Standing at the judgement" by Cheeks from 1959

Peacock 154 – "Heart and Soul" (1968) – Sensational Nightingales

Same lineup as Peacock 131 (1967)

* Johnson continues to write and render beautiful spiritual ballads such as "Another river," "Christians we are the ones" and "A better home"

Peacock 163 – "Songs of Rev. Julius Cheeks & The Night-

ingales" (1968) – Mighty Clouds of Joy

* This album is for the most part Little Joe and the Mighty Clouds covering the 'Gales' 1950s golden period. Cheeks leads on two remakes, "What would you give" and "Just a closer walk" and does a fine job

Peacock 1964 – "Rev. Julius Cheeks Sings" (1968)

* Astonishing album of fine work when considering Cheeks' physical condition. Tracks like "Get my child out of jail," "Same train" and "Waiting for my child" really stand out. Great overall performance mainly due to the fact that Cheeks was supported by the Four Gospel Knights, (circa. 1964-1968)

Peacock 166 – "The Super Groups" (1968) – Various Artists

* Includes two reissue songs by the Sensational Nightingales plus "Saints hold on" (1968) and "Brightly beams" (1968) – both lead by Charles Johnson

Peacock 175 – "It's Gonna Rain Again" – Sensational Nightingales (recorded 1969, issued 1972)

Same lineup as Peacock 131 (1967)

* Keeping to the 'Gale's signature style, Charles Johnson continues to lead fine songs, this time a bunch of mainly traditional hymns in a simple, soul-satisfaction manner. Superb renderings of "At the meeting," "A heart like Thine" and "At Calvary"

Peacock 177 – "You and I and Everyone" (1973) – Sensational Nightingales

Same lineup as Peacock 131 (1967)

* More hymn-based arrangements and close, high tenor singing using songs written and arranged by Johnson and Wallace and produced by Ira B. Tucker of the Dixie Hummingbirds. Winning songs include "You and I and everyone," "Face to face," and "I once was a stranger." Peacock had now been acquired by ABC-Dunhill Records

Peacock 190 – "Where Do I Go From Here" (1973) – Rev. Julius Cheeks

* Cheeks with his voice shot but still filled with enough spirit to move the place. 3 songs duplicate Peacock 164 (1968). Standouts include "Like a tramp on the street," "Bright light somewhere" (mis-titled), "Where do I go from here" and "Mountain railroad"

Peacock 197 – "I Know Not The Hour" (1974) – Sensational Nightingales

Same lineup as Peacock 131 (1967)

* The sixth collection from this solidly tight quartet -- the results of this offer us exquisite versions of Johnson's "Mother Mary and Joseph," Horace Thompson's beautiful "Nothing between" and Johnson's arrangement of "Love lifted me." Produced by Don Robey and Ira Tucker

Peacock ABC GLS 1974 – "The World's Greatest Gospel Artists Sing the Favorite Gospel Music of Our Time" (1973) – Various Artists

* This is a selection of 16 songs by 16 artists. The Sensational Nightingales are represented here with "My soul couldn't rest content" from Peacock LP 112 (1963) and by Rev. Julius Cheeks singing "Last mile of the way" (Peacock single 1875, 1963) -- this single side was only ever reissued on this album

Peacock ABC 59200 – "Gospel Artists Best" (1974) – Various Artists

* This collection includes "Brightly beams" by the 'Gales from Peacock LP 154 (1968)

Peacock ABC 59209 – "My Sisters and Brothers" (1974) – Sensational Nightingales

Same lineup as Peacock 131 (1967)

* More beautiful hymn book-like balladry -- "My sisters and brothers" and "Lift every voice and sing" fronted by Charles Johnson plus Jo Jo Wallace singing "If you strayed away" and Horace Thompson's pipes on "He'll make a way." Produced by Ira Tucker

Peacock ABC 59219 – "Almighty Hand" (1975) – Sensational Nightingales

Same lineup as Peacock 131 (1967)

* Truly glorious spiritual moments from this always dependable quartet. Favorites include "It's my desire," "Standing on the promises," "He hideth my soul" plus a sweet, long remake version of Cheeks' "What would you give" fronted by Johnson

Peacock ABC 59227 – "See You in the Rapture" (1976) – Sensational Nightingales

Same lineup as Peacock 131 (1967)

* A wonderful collection recorded at Quad in Pennsauken, N.J. Most pleasing songs include "See you in the rapture" and "Blessed Calvary" sung by Johnson and "Thank God I've been sealed" and "Oh how I love Jesus" perfected by Horace Thompson

Peacock ABC 59232 – "Jesus Is Coming" (1978) – Sensational Nightingales

Same lineup as Peacock 131 (1967)

* The most evenly recorded collection of gorgeous gospel hymns written by Johnson, Wallace and Thompson. Almost all the material is first rate. To pick 3 of the 6 winners out of 8 songs total, I would choose "Hard fighting soldier," "Learning to lean" and "Another river to cross." After thirteen years together, this winning lineup has reached beyond perfection

Malaco 4368 – "All About Jesus" (1980) – Sensational Nightingales

* With the same lineup gathered back in 1965, the 'Gales continue to stay with their old trademark sound which would help to explain why they have remained nationally successful. Beautiful renditions of "Crossroads of confusion," "Because He lives" and "Strayed away from God (Part 2)"

Malaco 4372 – "Saints Hold On" (1981) – Sensational Nightingales

With Rev. Haran Griffin on keyboards, Brian Williams on drums, Thompson on bass guitar as well as tenor, Jo Jo Wallace, tenor and guitar, Bill Woodruff, baritone and Charles Johnson, first lead, the ensemble excel on songs like "He just hung there," "My house is full" and "Savior don't pass me by"

Malaco 4380 – "He Is Real" (1982) – Sensational Nightingales

This is Charles Johnson's final album with the Sensational Nightingales. He was replaced by Calvert McNair from Briscoe, North Carolina sometime in 1983. He had formerly sung with Willie Banks and the Messengers. Many, many Johnson-lead gospel hymns measure up to the same soul-lifting standard as those of the past twenty years. Songs of special mention include "His hand in mine," "Do you know the man" and "When we walk with the Lord." Produced by Frank Williams of the Jackson Southernaires

Highly recommended is the wonderful DVD called "Live So God Can Use You." This DVD contains two concerts performed by the Sensational Nightingales and filmed by

601 Music (Malaco) in 1994, just before Bill Woodruff's passing. The DVD was issued in 2005 and can still be found on the Internet. There are nine songs, most led by Calvert McNair who replaced Charles Johnson in 1983. Unfortunately, these are two of McNair's last appearances as he too passed shortly after these recordings at the young age of 45. The high points of the collection include McNair's soulful, satisfying readings of "His Grace is sufficient" and the Charles Johnson-penned "Standing on the promises." Jo Jo introduces the selections as well as lead on a sermonette called "Whosoever will come" whereon he talks about some of his straying away from God during childhood and how his mother lead him to the light. McNair was a perfect replacement for Johnson.

What I found truly odd and something I had never seen before was that Bill Woodruff would often tap his feet and move his body in time with the rhythm and at the same moment clap out of time. Despite this minor oddity, the set is well worth the purchase. You will not find a long-serving gospel quartet singing and playing in a down-home style of the always traditional Sensational Nightingales. This kind of gospel singing is rarely found outside of the prevailing a cappella tradition.

For information concerning all of the later Sensational Nightingales Malaco album releases, please see the Malaco Records website, www.malaco.com

Malaco 4394 – No Man Can Stand Alone" (1984) – Charles Johnson & The Revivers

Opting to take up the Caucasian Pentecostal route with the

help of one Mr. Witten and the Better Way organization, Johnson packed up. Rick and Darrell Luster and the three formed the Reviveres. Johnson also played rhythm guitar. Darrell managed lead guitar and Rick handled the bass instrument. The album includes a slower remake of "Face to face" and a soul-soaked "We cannot stand alone." All are sung in a "no frills" style.

See end of discography for a more or less complete list of Revivers releases

The soldiers in the Sensational Nighingales stayed as one unit up to 1995 when Bill Woodruff passed on July 15th at the age of 76. He was replaced by Richard Luster. Almost a year after that, on May 4th, 1996, Calvert McNair left this life prematurely at the age of 45. He was replaced by lead vocalist Darrell Luster. Today's group includes Jo Jo Wallace, Thompson and Darrell Luster plus Larry Moore, lead and background singer.

Rev. Julius Cheeks – Later Group and Solo Album Discography

Su-Ann 1754 – "One of These Days We'll all Be Home" (1975 – Rev. Julius Cheeks

This was June's extremely rare comeback album after battling with alcohol and other problems. It contained eight songs. These included "Keep what I have and ask the Lord for more," "Live by the side of the road and be a friend to mankind" and "Right will win in the end" – all three are

June's compositions. The remaining are old, traditional gospel charts. Having never been able to turn up a copy, I cannot comment on them.

Savoy 14486 – "How Far is Heaven" (1978) – The Living Legend – Rev. Julius Cheeks & The Four Knights

This album is an effort to revive the glory days of the early 1960s when "June" and the Knights tore up the churches. Sadly, the only remaining visual record of this period is from TV Gospel time Program 33, filmed in Baltimore on September 5th, 1964. The group appeared with Jessie Mae Renfro and sang "Morning train," "Mother sang these songs" and "Great change in me."

On this album he grinds out a good remake of "Last mile of the way" and "See how they done my Lord" with the group along with his wife on piano, and his niece, soloist Genobia Jeter, showing up on one selection. The standard here does not really quite match that of TV Gospel Time #33.

Savoy 14504 – "Family Reunion" (1979) – Julius Cheeks featuring Jenoba (not Genobia) Jeter & Addia Jeter (June's sister)

Very nicely produced and performed collection with notable performances of June and Jenoba on the title track, active solo effort on "Don't drive me away" plus June's "Journey to the sky" and remake of "Where do I go from here"

Savoy 7040 (2 Vol. set) – "We'll Lay Down Our Lives For The Lord" (1979) – Rev. Julius Cheeks and the Young Adult Choir with featured soloists plus the Modulations Live

Fine performances from Cheeks and Genobia, Marguerite Jeter, Glenn Jones and the Modulations. His third finest album collection after Peacock 101 (1959) and Peacock 164 (1968). All three are essential

Savoy 14554 – "Somebody Left On That Morning Train" (1980) – Rev. Julius Cheeks

More strongly convicted attempts to put over the might of his religion on the title track and duets with Marguerite, Genobia and Addie Jeter. Produced by Rev. Milton Biggham

Savoy 14608 – "At The Gate I Know" (Live) (1981) – Rev. Julius Cheeks – The Legend Lives On

This fine tribute collection album came out shortly after June's death. He passed in Miami on January 21st, 1981.

The set includes very fine last-ditch renderings of "At the gate I know," "Crying in the chapel" and "I want to go where Jesus is" – first recorded with the 'Gales in 1959. There is also an outstanding duet with George McAllister, a fine singer. All in all a great send-off for the great soul who changed the course of confessional music both in the church and on gospel's chitlin' circuit.

Listing of Most Revivers Albums with Charles Johnson

Malaco 4394 (1984) – "No Man Can Stand Alone"
With the Luster Brothers – Darrell and Ricky

Gloryland (1986) – "There Is A Guarantee In Jesus"
Betterway 2850 (1988) – "One Night Revival"
Betterway 2394 (1989) – "Sealed 'Til The Day Of Redemption"
Betterway 2911 (1989) – Mansion Over The Hilltop"
Betterway 3287 (1990) – He Hideth My Soul"
Betterway 4076 (1990) – "Until Then"
Betterway 5122 (1991) – "The Time Is Drawing Nigh"
Canaan 701523536 (1992) – "Let's Have Church" (also on video cassette)
Canaan 7019532535 (1994) – "We Cannot Stand Alone"
Above with Gary Miles, Melvin Wilson and Greg Logins

Canaan 7019538533 (1995) – "I Believe"
Above with Michael Watts and Tracy Pierce

Centergy Music (1996) – "Hymns"
Spring Hill 5444 (1997) – "Good Time In The House"
Above with Joe Yancey, vocals and drums, Steve Boyd, vocals and keyboards, Maurice Morgan Snr., vocals and lead guitar, and Tracy Pierce, vocals and bass guitar

Centergy Music (1999) – "Waiting For The Messiah"
Custom (2004) – "Reach Down And Touch Me"
Custom (2005) – "20th Anniversary"
Five Stones (2005) – "Christmas With Charles Johnson & The Revivers"

The Revivers' farewell concert took place in October 2011. The group then broke up

Highlights of The Sensational Nightingales' Later Career

1983 Interviewed and selected as gospel ambassadors on the International Cultural Arts Exchange program through the U.S. Information Agency

Performed at the Bern & Villingen Festivals in Switzerland and Germany

1984 First overseas tours sponsored by I.C.A.E. 2 months spent touring in Sierra Leone, Ivory Coast, Ghana, Zimbabwe, Botswana, Zambia, Zaire, Congo (Cameroon) and onto Europe (France, Switzerland, Germany & Spain)

Appeared at various festivals: Switzerland at the "American Spiritual & Gospel Festival" with the Stars of Faith, Barrett Sisters and Rev. Robert Mayes. Also appeared at the Montreux, Berlin & Vienna Festivals and at the Hague (Northsea) Festival

1984-85 Best selling album "I Surrender All" makes it onto the Billboard Top Spirituals Albums list and stays on the chart for 2 months

1987-91 Toured European Continent on a regular basis. Summer Festival appearances include Marcillac (France), Northsea (Netherlands), Montauban (Bretagne,

France), Lugano (Switzerland), Carthage (Tunisia), Monaster (Tunisia), Wetzler (West Germany), Paray-Le-Monial (France) and Brugge (Belgium.) They appeared at countless concert halls where they sang, gave lectures and talked about the history of gospel quartet. They also appeared on radio and television in Western Europe

1992 Made their first I.C.A.E. trip to the islands of the Caribbean

Early
1990s Highlights: Appearances at the Sacred Arts Festival of the City of Paris, the Liege guitar Festival (Belgium), The Cully Jazz Festival 1, Paris Gospel Festival, Jazz En Touraine (France) and the Bern International Festival (Switzerland)

1995 Jo Jo Wallace honored for his achievements by Bill Clinton at the White House

1998 Sensational Nightingales become first quartet to be inducted into the American Gospel Music Hall of Fame in Detroit

2003 Sensational Nightingales nominated for best traditional soul-gospel album – "Songs To Edify" during 46th Annual Grammy Awards

Gave prestigious performances at the Madrid National Auditorium, at Stephansdon in Vienna and at the Linz Cathedral (Austria)

2011 Brother Wallace Day, given by Pastor K.R. Hammond at the Union Baptist Church in Durham, N.C. – a day of honor bestowed on Jo Jo Wallace for his work for the church and around the globe with the Sensational Nightingales.

The Wallace Scholarship Fund was set up in Durham by Lillian Bowser.

Jo Jo Wallace awarded a Capitol Citation from Elaine F. Marshall, Secretary of State

2013   The Sensational Nightingales celebrate their 67th anniversary Appreciation at Durham's Armory on Morgan & Foster Streets, with the Disciples of NYC and the Swanee Quintet of Augusta, Georgia

Jo Jo is coming up to his 89th birthday and by all accounts is good for a few more years. His bright and sunny, positive attitude to life has certainly helped carry him through many rough spots. He still considers himself, like a soldier on call, in reserve, ready to go out and sing and play as he has done for most of his life. When he is off the road he is either puttering around in his vegetable patch or out doing what he likes doing best, going fishing.

Further Sources of Information on Sensational Nightingales

National Tribute Dinner Booklet, Nov. 1992 with monographs of Sensational Nightingales at that time

"Standing At The Judgement" – Seamus McGarvey, The Gospel Spot in Living Blues Magazine, 2005. Brief history of the Sensational Nightingales

"The Charles Johnson Story" – Opal Louis Nations, Real Blues Magzine #5, February/March 1997. Life history of Charles Johnson up to Revivers

"The Enduring Song of the Sensational Nightingales" – Edwin Smith, Rejoice Magazine, February / March 1992. Interview and brief history

"The Twist – The Story of the Song and Dance That Changed the World" – Jim Dawson, 1995. The Wallace / Woodruff part in composing the song

Bro. Joseph "Jo Jo" Wallace interview by Melanie Credle. Herald Sun, Durham, N.C., Dec. 1992. Some highlights from Jo Jo's life

"From Thomas A. Dorsey to Jay Leno, A Brief History of Gospel Music" – Opal Louis Nations. Lecture notes from Johnny Otis's Vista College lecture, Feb. 2003

"Sensational Nightingales" Were Really Sensational – Cam-news / The Cameroon Tribune, Dec. 5th, 1984. Write-up of concert at Yaounde Conference Center

Sensational Nightingales publicity flyer and brief history by Willie Leiser, International Booking Agency, Montreux, Switzerland, 1995

Encyclopedia of Early American Vocal Groups (1858-1950) – Douglas E. Friedman & Anthony J. Gribin. Harmony Songs Publications, 2013

"Fathers of Soul," Chapter 7, "The Gospel Sound" – Anthony Heilbut, Limelight Editions (Revised), 1985. Bios of Cheeks and Rev. Claude Jeter

"The Sound of Philadelphia" – Tony Cummings – Methuen, England, 1975

"How I Got Over --The Ward Singers" – Willa Ward & Toni Rose – Temple University, 1997

"Duke / Peacock Records" – Galen Gart & Roy C. Ames – Big Nickel Pubs., 1990

"Great God A'Mighty – The Dixie Hummingbirds" – Jerry Zolten, Oxford U., 2003

"The Things We Used To Do – Selah Jubilee Singers," Chapter 4, Group Harmony – Todd R. Baptista, TRB Enterprises, 2000

CHARLES JOHNSON

Charles Johnson, lead singer, writer and arranger for the Sensational Nightingales & Revivers gospel groups, passed away around 1:30 a.m. Monday October 6th, 2014 of a massive heart attack. Funeral services were held on Monday October 13th at Mt. Zion Christian Church in his home town of Durham, North Carolina.

ABOUT THE AUTHOR

Opal Louis Nations was born in Brighton, England. During the mid-sixties he worked as lead vocalist in London clubs with the late Alexis Korner's Band and later his own group, The Frays. He helped popularize American soul-based R & B and gospel music in Great Britain. It was through his efforts that black American gospel artists visited the country to perform in various major cities. He also became part of one of England's first integrated gospel groups, The Ram John Holder Group. With The Frays, and later as a soloist, he recorded for Decca Records in London. After brief periods with various London R&B bands, he turned his back on singing and began a career as an experimental fiction writer. His textual work, sometimes strange, sometimes humorous in nature, appeared in over 200 small press magazines around the world. Texts have been translated and published in French, German, and Norwegian. He is the author of over thirty books of fiction, drawings, and collage. As an editor of his own press, Strange Faeces, he brought to the public's attention fresh young poets and writers, both in the publication of books and through his literary magazine periodical, *Strange Faeces*. He was awarded The Perpetua and Pushcart Prizes for his fiction. Some of his sound-poems have been included in the T.V. series *Man and His Music,* a globally syndicated program hosted by Yehudi Menhuin. In the late 70's he became interested in radio, and with The Radio Lux Players of Vancouver helped script and perform in many independently produced radio plays. After moving to Oakland, Ca. in 1981, he joined KPFA in Berkeley where for 10 years he hosted an R&B / Gospel show -- *Doo- Wop Delights* and, later, *Rockin' at Midnite*, as well as a world music program, *Harmonia Mundi.* After 14 years' tenure with KPFA, he hosted a two-hour traditional gospel program at KUSP in Santa Cruz called *In the Heavenly Way.* He produced the Legendary Gospel Specialty reissue series for Fantasy Records in Berkeley and the Nashboro Gospel reissue series for AVI in Los Angeles. He currently spends his time interviewing gospel performers, writing articles on a regular basis for *Blues & Rhythm* and *Doctor Jazz* (to name a few) and conducting music research for CD reissues on the Ace, Jasmine and JSP labels, among others.

*Some other **Black Scat Books** you'll enjoy:*

Made in the USA
Lexington, KY
11 September 2016